V   5

THE POCKET REFERENCE

Mella Mincberg

Osborne **McGraw-Hill**

Berkeley New York St. Louis San Francisco
Auckland Bogotá Hamburg London Madrid
Mexico City Milan Montreal New Delhi Panama City
Paris São Paulo Singapore Sydney
Tokyo Toronto

Osborne **McGraw-Hill**
2600 Tenth Street
Berkeley, California 94710
U.S.A.

For information on translations or book distributors outside of the U.S.A.,
please write to Osborne **McGraw-Hill** at the above address.

WordPerfect 6: The Pocket Reference

Contributing Editor: Leigh Yafa
Acquisitions Editor: Jeffrey Pepper
Associate Editor: Bob Myren
Technical Editor: Jim Sheldon
Project Editor: Madhu Prasher
Copy Editor: Judith Brown
Proofreader: Scott Brown
Indexer: Valerie Robbins
Computer Designers: J. E. Christgau, Mickey Galicia
Cover Design: Compass Marketing

1234567890 DOC 99876543

ISBN 0-07-881905-9

CONTENTS

Introduction

This pocket reference is a concise, comprehensive source for information on WordPerfect version 6.0. It is for the beginning or advanced user who is familiar with how WordPerfect operates but requires either a refresher on exactly what certain features accomplish or a keystroke-by-keystroke handbook.

There are two main sections to this reference guide. The first section, "General Reminders," provides abbreviated instructions on how to successfully use WordPerfect and its powerful features. Topics include how to start and end a WordPerfect session; methods for moving the cursor, editing text, and altering a document's format; and procedures for saving, retrieving, printing, and working in multiple document windows.

The first section also includes tables of pull-down menus, function and shortcut keys, and keystrokes for moving the cursor and deleting text. Use these tables whenever you need a quick reminder on how to perform basic WordPerfect tasks.

The second section, "Features and Commands," an alphabetical list, comprises the bulk of this reference guide and presents a comprehensive list of WordPerfect's features in alphabetical order. It provides the command sequence required to activate each feature along with an explanation of that feature's purpose and applications.

The following conventions are used throughout this pocket reference:

- Items on WordPerfect's menu system are listed in the order in which they are chosen. They are separated by commas with their mnemonic letters underlined. For instance, File, Open means to choose the File menu and then choose the Open item from that menu. You may use either the mouse or the keyboard to make your selection. If you use the keyboard, you can use the mnemonic letters to do so. Any alternative method for executing the same command will follow in parentheses, such as File, Exit (F7).

- A plus sign between two keystrokes indicates that the keys must be pressed simultaneously. For instance, CTRL+END means that while holding down the CTRL key you press END and then release both keys.

- A comma between two keystrokes indicates that they must be pressed sequentially. For instance, HOME, SPACEBAR means that you press HOME, release it, and then press SPACEBAR.

Quick answers are easy to find with this pocket reference. If you should require more in-depth information on the WordPerfect program, refer to additional Osborne/McGraw-Hill sources, such as *WordPerfect 6 Made Easy*, also written by Mella Mincberg.

General Reminders

This section describes the procedures you should keep in mind to work effectively with WordPerfect and avoid potential problems.

STARTING AND ENDING A WORDPERFECT SESSION

When you get WordPerfect to run on your computer, this procedure is referred to as *starting* or *loading* WordPerfect. The process for exiting WordPerfect is just as critical.

Starting WordPerfect

To begin a WordPerfect session, turn on your computer as you usually do. When the DOS prompt appears (for example, C> or C:\>), you are ready to load WordPerfect. To load WordPerfect from DOS, follow these steps:

1. If you are not located on the drive where the WordPerfect program files are located, switch to that drive by typing the drive name (for example, **c:**), then press ENTER.

2. Type **wp** and press ENTER. If WordPerfect 6.0 begins to load, then do nothing more, and wait for the WordPerfect document window to appear. If, instead, the computer displays the message "Bad command or file name", proceed to step 3.

3. Type **cd \wp6O** and press ENTER. This switches to the directory where the WordPerfect program files are located. (If you or your installer created a directory for the WordPerfect program files with a name other than WP60, you will have to substitute the correct directory name after you type **cd **.)

4. Type **wp** and press ENTER to start WordPerfect 6.0.

Another option is to load WordPerfect from the WordPerfect Shell. The Shell is a separate program that is included with WordPerfect 6.0. The Shell lets you load applications and work with more than one application at the same time. You can load WordPerfect 6.0 from the Shell by double-clicking on the program name or by using the arrow keys to move to the program name, highlighting it, and pressing ENTER. Refer to SHELL, EXIT TO in the "Features and Commands" section for more on the Shell.

Once WordPerfect is loaded, you are ready to type, edit, save, and print your documents. Refer to DEFAULT DRIVE/DIRECTORY, CHANGE in the "Features and Commands" section if you want the majority of your files to be stored in or retrieved from a directory other than the WPDOCS directory that was created during the installation process.

Error Messages on Startup

The most common error message you may encounter when loading WordPerfect is "Backup File Exists." This message appears if, during your most recent WordPerfect working session, you experienced a power or machine failure or turned off the computer without exiting WordPerfect properly (described next). In the error message dialog box, you will be given the option to rename, delete, or open the backup file. (See BACKUP in the "Features and Commands" section.)

Other error messages may be an indication of an improper installation of the program or the need for a special startup option. Refer to STARTUP OPTIONS in the "Features and Commands" section.

Exiting from WordPerfect

Always exit WordPerfect properly before you turn off your computer. This allows the program to close its own temporary files, which are created each time you start up WordPerfect. To exit from WordPerfect, you have several options.

WordPerfect allows you to work on up to nine documents at once. When only one document window is open, use these steps to exit WordPerfect:

1. Choose File, Exit (F7).

2. Either choose Yes to save the document that is onscreen, in which case you must indicate a filename, or choose No to exit without saving the document.

3. Choose Yes to exit WordPerfect.

When one or more document windows are open, there is an alternative method that lets you exit all the document windows at once:

1. Choose File, Exit WP (HOME, F7).

2. Choose the letter or click the check box of those files for which you wish to change the Save/Don't Save status. An X should appear in the check box of any documents you wish to save. You can also choose (Un)mark to toggle between Save/Don't Save for all the open documents at once.

3. Choose Save and Exit (or choose Exit if you indicated that you did not wish to save any open documents) by clicking this item or pressing the ENTER key.

4. WordPerfect will request a filename for each document you wish to save that hasn't been saved previously. After you indicate filenames, WordPerfect will save the files and exit.

Once you see the DOS prompt onscreen, you are ready to turn off your computer or start another software program. Or, if you started WordPerfect from the Shell, you should now be located at the Shell menu.

THE THREE VIEW MODES

You may choose from among three display modes when working with your documents: text mode, graphics mode, and page mode. It is possible to switch to any of the three modes during the same editing session. To change the view mode, you can either choose <u>V</u>iew and select the desired mode, or press CTRL+F3 and then choose the desired mode.

In text mode, documents are displayed in monospaced characters of the same size regardless of the fonts chosen, and the contents of graphics and equation boxes are not displayed. Thus, text mode does not accurately reflect the format of the printed document. In addition, graphics and equation boxes cannot be moved or resized with the mouse when working in text mode.

Text mode is not as visually exciting as the other two modes, but it is by far the fastest mode to work in since it doesn't require as much memory as the other view modes. Also, your screen will not have to be redrawn as frequently as with the other modes. You may find it very efficient to enter data in text mode and then switch to another mode to refine the document, particularly when working with complex documents containing many font changes and graphic elements. Also, use text mode if your computer has limited memory or does not have graphics capability.

In graphics mode, WordPerfect will attempt to display the fonts you have selected on the screen. The contents of graphics and equation boxes will also be displayed. This mode is often referred to as WYSIWYG or "what you see is what you get." In other words, the document on the screen will closely resemble the printed document. Drag and Drop editing is available in graphics mode, and screen elements such as the Button Bar can be displayed as icons (pictures) instead of text.

Page mode is very similar to graphics mode, but is more flexible. In addition to WYSIWYG and Drag and Drop editing capabilities, page mode also allows you to see document headers, footers, and footnotes on the editing screen.

Graphics and page mode are dependent on the Zoom feature, which specifies the magnitude with which text is displayed. See ZOOM in the "Features and Commands" section for more details.

TYPING TEXT

As you type a document in WordPerfect, it is important to allow WordPerfect to determine where the lines should end in a paragraph. When your cursor reaches the right margin, WordPerfect automatically advances your cursor to the next line. This is referred to as *word wrap*. Do not press the ENTER key at the end of every line. Only press the ENTER key to:

- End a paragraph
- End a short line of text (such as a title)
- Insert a blank line

Also, use the TAB key to indent the first line in a paragraph. The line will be indented half an inch (unless you change the tab stop locations). The SPACEBAR should not be used. It is unreliable for indenting because the position and width of spaces can change.

USING THE MOUSE

In WordPerfect, a mouse can perform every task except typing text. You operate a mouse by moving it to control the whereabouts of your mouse pointer onscreen. If you are using the mouse in text mode, the mouse pointer is represented by a small, colored (or reverse video) rectangle. If you are using a mouse in graphics or page mode, the mouse pointer is represented by a small arrow.

In WordPerfect, the left mouse button is the principal button. The terminology for using a mouse is as follows:

Point	Move the mouse until the mouse pointer rests on an item.
Click	Press and release the mouse button.
Double-click	Press and release the mouse button twice in rapid succession.
Drag	While holding down on the mouse button, move the mouse.

MOVING THE CURSOR

Once you've typed a document onscreen, WordPerfect offers a myriad of methods for moving the cursor and scrolling through your text. You can use either a mouse or the keyboard's cursor movement keypad.

When using a mouse, move the mouse pointer onscreen to the location where you wish to relocate the cursor and click the left mouse button. Or, you can click and hold the right mouse button and drag the mouse up or down to scroll through the text. You can also use the mouse in combination with the vertical and horizontal scroll bars to scroll through the text and move the cursor. (See SCROLL BARS in the "Features and Commands" section.)

When you use the cursor movement keypad, the keys you employ depend on where you wish to move the cursor, as shown in the following tables.

Cursor Movement Left and Right

Key Sequence	Cursor Movement
←	One character left
→	One character right
CTRL+←	One word left
CTRL+→	One word right
HOME, ←	Left edge of screen
HOME, →	Right edge of screen

Key Sequence	Cursor Movement
HOME, HOME, ← or END	Left edge of line (useful if the line is longer than the width of the screen)
HOME, HOME, → or END	Right edge of line (useful if the line is longer than the width of the screen)
HOME, HOME, HOME, ←	Left edge of line before codes
HOME, HOME, HOME, →	Right edge of line after codes

Cursor Movement Up and Down

Key Sequence	Cursor Movement
↑	One line up
↓	One line down
– (numeric keypad) or HOME, ↑	Top line on screen (or next screen up if cursor is on top line)
+ (numeric keypad) or HOME, ↓	Bottom line on screen (or next screen down if cursor is on bottom line)
PGUP	Top of previous page
PGDN	Top of next page
HOME, HOME, ↑	Beginning of document
HOME, HOME, ↓	End of document
HOME, HOME, HOME, ↑	Beginning of document before codes
HOME, HOME, HOME, ↓	End of document after codes

Cursor Movement with Go To (CTRL+HOME) in Standard Text

Key Sequence	Cursor Movement
CTRL+HOME, *letter/symbol*	Next occurrence of that letter or symbol within the next 2000 characters
CTRL+HOME, ENTER	Next hard return character
CTRL+HOME, ↑	Top of current page
CTRL+HOME, ↓	Bottom of current page
CTRL+HOME, #	Top of specified page number (#)
CTRL+HOME, ALT+F4	Beginning of blocked text (Highlight will be removed)
CTRL+HOME, CTRL+HOME	Cursor position before last cursor movement command

Cursor Movement with Go To (CTRL+HOME) in Text Columns and Tables

Key Sequence	Cursor Movement
CTRL+HOME, ←	Previous column or cell
CTRL+HOME, →	Next column or cell
CTRL+HOME, HOME, ←	Leftmost column or cell
CTRL+HOME, HOME, →	Rightmost column or cell
CTRL+HOME, ↑	First line of current column or cell
CTRL+HOME, ↓	Last line of current column or cell
CTRL+HOME, HOME, ↑	First cell in column (tables only)
CTRL+HOME, HOME, ↓	Last cell in column (tables only)

Key Sequence	Cursor Movement
CTRL+HOME, HOME, HOME, ↑	First cell in table (tables only)
CTRL+HOME, HOME, HOME, ↓	Last cell in table (tables only)
CTRL+HOME, *cell address*	Specified cell (must be in table edit mode, tables only)

EDITING A DOCUMENT

Once you know how to move the cursor through a document, you are ready to edit text. The editing method you employ depends on the changes that are necessary. To insert text, simply position the cursor and begin typing. If you are in Insert mode, existing text will move to the right to accommodate the new characters you type. In Typeover mode, existing text will be replaced by the new characters you type. The INS key controls this Insert/Typeover option. (See INSERT MODE and TYPEOVER MODE in the "Features and Commands" section.) To delete text, the keys you press depend on the amount of text you wish to erase, as described in the following table.

Deletion Options

Key Sequence	Text Deleted
BACKSPACE	Character left of cursor
DEL	Character at cursor (or to right of cursor if using graphics mode)
CTRL+BACKSPACE or CTRL+DEL	Word at cursor
HOME, BACKSPACE	Characters left to word boundary
HOME, DEL	Characters right to word boundary, including trailing space
CTRL+END	Characters right to line end
CTRL+PGDN	Characters from cursor to page end

Key Sequence	Text Deleted
Block text, DEL or BACKSPACE	Characters/codes in highlighted block
ESC	Previous deletion restored (see UNDELETE in the "Features and Commands" section)

ACTIVATING FEATURES

WordPerfect's features are accessed in various ways. You can issue a command from the pull-down menu bar, or you can bypass the menu bar with function keys and other shortcut key combinations, or with the Button Bar feature.

Pull-Down Menus

WordPerfect's menu system is accessed from the menu bar at the top of the screen. Nine menus are listed, as follows:

File   Edit   View   Layout   Tools   Font   Graphics
Window   Help

To "pull down" a menu from the menu bar with the mouse, simply point to the desired menu and click the left mouse button. Similarly, to choose an item from this menu, point to and click the item.

When using the keyboard, hold the ALT key while typing the mnemonic letter for the desired menu. Then choose a menu item by pressing the mnemonic letter for that item. For example, to display the File menu, press ALT+F. Then to choose the Open item from that menu, press O.

You can also browse through the menu bar before you choose from it. With the mouse, you can drag across the menu bar or within menus using the left mouse button to see the selections on the menus. With the keyboard, you can activate the pull-down menus by pressing ALT+= , and then use the LEFT ARROW and RIGHT ARROW keys to move between menus and the UP ARROW and DOWN ARROW keys to move within a menu.

There are subtle cues on the menu bar that are designed to help you anticipate what will happen after you make a menu selection:

- If a menu item is followed by an ellipsis (three dots), WordPerfect will require further information from you in order to fulfill your request. You will be presented with a dialog box so that you can communicate with WordPerfect.

- If a menu item has an arrow to the right of the selection, you will be presented with a submenu.

- If a menu item has no mark beside it, the command will be executed without further input from you.

- Certain menu items may appear dimmed, indicating that the features are not available to you based upon the current status of the document. For instance, if you have an empty document window, many of the items on the Edit menu will be unavailable since there is nothing blocked in the document to cut, copy, or otherwise edit.

The pull-down menus and the features assigned to each of them are shown here.

File	Edit	View
New	Undo	Text Mode
Open	Undelete	Graphics Mode
Retrieve	Repeat	Page Mode
Close	Cut and Paste	Reveal Codes
Save	Copy and Paste	Ribbon
Save As	Cut	Outline Bar
File Manager	Copy	Pull-Down Menus
Master Document	Paste	Button Bar
Compare Documents	Append	Button Bar Setup
Summary	Block	Zoom

File (*contd.*)

Setup
Print/Fax
Print Preview
Go To Shell
Exit
Exit WP

Edit (*contd.*)

Select
Convert Case
Search
Replace
Bookmark
Go To

View (*contd.*)

Horizontal Scroll Bar
Vertical Scroll Bar
Screen Setup

Layout

Character
Line
Page
Document
Columns
Tables
Envelope
Special Codes
Other
Margins
Justification
Tab Set
Alignment
Header/Footer/
   Watermark
Footnote
Endnote
Comment
Styles

Tools

Writing Tools
Macro
Outline
Merge
Sort
Date
Index
Table of Contents
List
Cross-Reference
Table of
   Authorities
Generate
Math
Spreadsheet
Hypertext
Sound Clip

Font

Font
Normal
Size/Position
Bold
Underline
Double Underline
Italics
Outline
Shadow
Small Caps
Redline
Strikeout
Print Color
WP Characters
Hidden Text

Graphics

Retrieve Image
Graphics Boxes
Graphics Lines

Window

Minimize
Frame
Maximize

Help

Contents
Index
How Do I

Graphics (*contd.*)	Window (*contd.*)	Help (*contd.*)
Borders	Tile	Coaches
Fill Styles	Cascade	Macros
Line Draw	Next	Tutorial
	Previous	WP Info
	Switch	
	Switch To	

Function Keys and Other Shortcut Keys

You can access a feature by pressing a function key (labeled F1 through F12) either by itself or in combination with the CTRL, ALT, or SHIFT key. The WordPerfect program is packaged with a keyboard template that indicates which function key controls which special feature(s). Be sure to place the template next to the function keys.

Here is a list of the features assigned to function keys:

Feature	Function Key Combination
BLOCK	ALT+F4 or F12
BOLD	F6
BOOKMARK	SHIFT+F12
CENTER	SHIFT+F6
COLUMNS/TABLES	ALT+F7
DATE	SHIFT+F5
END FIELD	F9
ENVELOPE	ALT+F12
EXIT	F7
EXIT WP	HOME, F7
FILE MANAGER	F5
FLUSH RIGHT	ALT+F6
FONT	CTRL+F8
FOOTNOTE	CTRL+F7

Feature	Function Key Combination
FORMAT	SHIFT+F8
GRAPHICS	ALT+F9
HELP	F1
INDENT ->	F4
INDENT -><-	SHIFT+F4
MACRO PLAY	ALT+F10
MACRO RECORD	CTRL+F10
MARK TEXT	ALT+F5
MERGE CODES	SHIFT+F9
MERGE/SORT	CTRL+F9
MOVE	CTRL+F4
OPEN/RETRIEVE	SHIFT+F10
OUTLINE	CTRL+F5
PRINT/FAX	SHIFT+F7
REPLACE	ALT+F2
REVEAL CODES	ALT+F3 or F11
SAVE	CTRL+F12
SAVE AS	F10
SCREEN	CTRL+F3
SEARCH ->	F2
SEARCH <-	SHIFT+F2
SETUP	SHIFT+F1
SHELL	CTRL+F1
SPELL	CTRL+F2
STYLE	ALT+F8
SWITCH	SHIFT+F3
SWITCH TO DOC	F3
TAB ALIGN	CTRL+F6
TAB SET	CTRL+F11
TABLE EDIT	ALT+F11
UNDERLINE	F8

Feature	Function Key Combination
WP CHARACTERS	SHIFT+F11
WRITING TOOLS	ALT+F1

Besides the shortcuts using the function keys, there are additional shortcut keys that are combinations of the CTRL key plus a letter (or sometimes another key). For example, a shortcut for undoing your last editing action is CTRL+Z. To activate this feature, hold down the CTRL key and, while holding it down, press Z. Then release both keys.

Here is a list of features assigned to shortcut key combinations:

Feature	Key Combination
BOLD	CTRL+B
COMPOSE	CTRL+A
COPY	CTRL+C
COPY AND PASTE	CTRL+INS
CUT	CTRL+X
CUT AND PASTE	CTRL+DEL
FIND QUICKMARK	CTRL+F
HARD PAGE BREAK	CTRL+ENTER
ITALICS	CTRL+I
NORMAL FONT	CTRL+N
OUTLINE EDIT	CTRL+O
PAGE NUMBER (FORMATTED)	CTRL+P
PASTE	CTRL+V
PLAY SOUND CLIP	CTRL+S
RECORD SOUND CLIP	CTRL+D
REPEAT	CTRL+R
SET QUICKMARK	CTRL+Q
TOGGLE TEXT or PARAGRAPH NUMBER	CTRL+T
UNDERLINE	CTRL+U

Feature	Key Combination
UNDO	CTRL+Z
WP CHARACTERS	CTRL+W

Button Bar

The Button Bar lets you choose features with the click of a button. The button bar can be displayed at the top of the document, and you can place on that bar various buttons for all the features that you use often. You must use a mouse to take advantage of this feature. See BUTTON BAR in the "Features and Commands" section for more information.

WordPerfect Actions and Codes

After issuing a command—either by choosing a pull-down menu item, pressing a shortcut key, or clicking the Button Bar—read the onscreen messages carefully for an indication of what to do next. The possibilities include

- WordPerfect presents a dialog box that lists various choices. To select dialog box options, use the TAB key to move from one option to another and/or press the mnemonic character associated with the menu item; or position the mouse pointer on the desired item and click the left mouse button. (If the desired option is already highlighted, you may press ENTER or click the right mouse button to select it.)

- WordPerfect reveals a submenu of a pull-down menu. Choose a submenu item in the same way that you choose a pull-down menu item.

- WordPerfect performs the action without any more input from you.

- WordPerfect performs the action by inserting a code, as is the case, for example, when you choose the Bold, Center, Flush Right, Tab Align, or Underline commands; a feature has now been activated.

Codes are hidden in the document window; they are displayed only when you use the Reveal Codes feature. Choose View, Reveal Codes. In the Reveal Codes window, codes are displayed in boldface and surrounded by square brackets. There are two types of codes: paired and open.

As the name implies, *paired codes* come in twos, with an On code that marks the location where a feature is turned on and an Off code that marks the location where the feature is turned off; for example, [Bold On] and [Bold Off]. Paired codes are commonly those that alter a font attribute.

Open codes are single codes that turn on a feature from the code location either to the end of the document or to the location where another code of the same type has been inserted. An example is [Ln Spacing:2]. Open codes are commonly codes that format lines or pages in the document.

Canceling a Feature, Menu, or Dialog Box

To cancel a menu or dialog box, press the ESC key, click the middle mouse button or choose Cancel (from a dialog box). You may have to press ESC more than once to completely back out of a menu. To cancel a feature immediately after inserting a code, you can display the Reveal Codes screen, make sure your cursor is located to the right of the code you wish to remove, and press the BACKSPACE key. This will erase the code and thus turn off the feature.

CUSTOMIZING WORDPERFECT AND CHANGING A DOCUMENT'S FORMAT

The WordPerfect program was designed with default settings that control how certain features should operate, how your WordPerfect document window appears, and

how all new documents should be formatted. You can
permanently alter these default settings; refer to
INITIAL CODES, FONT, SCREEN SETUP, and SETUP in
the "Features and Commands" section for further details.

Altering default settings for how documents are
formatted will only affect documents created after the
changes are made. Existing documents will continue to
conform to the settings present at the time they were
created, unless they are retrieved into another document.

You can change a variety of default format settings at
any time and as many times as desired for a single
document. To change the format for the document
onscreen, use the Layout menu.

Each time you change a specific format setting, a code is
inserted into the document. The Automatic Code
Placement feature helps you to place formatting codes in
the appropriate locations. Top and bottom margin codes,
for instance, are placed at the top of the page, while left
and right margin codes are placed at the beginning of
the current paragraph. See AUTO CODE PLACEMENT in
the "Features and Commands" section.

To abort a format change, you can use the Layout menu
to reset it again. Or, you can use the Reveal Codes
feature to find and delete the hidden code you inserted.

When working in text mode, the effect of many of
WordPerfect's formatting features (such as full
justification) will not be visible in the document window.
In addition, font changes will not be accurately reflected.
Use the Reveal Codes feature to verify that the feature
has been activated, or use the Print Preview feature to
see on the screen how the document will appear when
printed (as described in PRINT PREVIEW in the "Features
and Commands" section). You may also switch to
graphics mode or page mode to see the effect of
formatting and font changes.

Blocking Text

You can apply certain formatting and font changes to a
specific portion of text. To do so, first use the Block

feature or a mouse to highlight that text. You are then ready to change the font, line spacing, margins, or other formatting only for the highlighted text. (See BLOCK and MOUSE in the "Features and Commands" section.)

Be aware that some features may behave differently when activated with the Block feature on. For example, on the pull-down menus, you may notice that some items such as Cut, Copy, and Paste appear in dimmed text, signifying that the items cannot be selected at the present time because of the status of the Block feature. Certain items can be selected only with Block on, while others can be selected only with Block off.

OPENING, SAVING, AND MANAGING DOCUMENTS

When you first start WordPerfect you are presented with a blank screen, ready for you to begin typing a new document. You can bring files from disk into the document window. Conversely, you can save a copy of your work into a file on disk.

Bringing Files onto the Screen

You can open an existing file and place it in a clear document window. Choose File, Open and, in the Open Document dialog box, type the name of the file you wish to open, including its location (for example C:\WPDOCS\MYFILE.1), and choose OK. If you are not sure of the name and location of the file, you can use the File Manager or Quicklist to browse through directory listings. (See FILE MANAGER and QUICKLIST in the "Features and Commands" section.)

Retrieving a file assumes that you wish to combine the file you request with the file already in the active document window. In the active document, place your cursor where the text from the second file should appear. Choose File, Retrieve. In the Retrieve Document dialog

box, type the name and location of the file to be
retrieved. Choose OK.

Saving Files to Disk

To save a file for the first time, choose File, Save As. In
the Save As dialog box, type the name of the document
and choose OK.

Documents are stored on disk in a file with a filename of
your choosing. A filename can contain one to eight
characters, including letters, numbers, and the following
symbols:

! @ # $ % ^ & ( ) - { } _ '

The filename can also have an optional filename
extension, which is separated from the filename by a
period (.) and can contain one to three characters.

Examples of acceptable filenames are MEMO, MEMO1,
MEMO.1, MEMO1.HBJ, and MEMO#1.HBJ. It is
important to remember that a filename cannot contain
spaces.

To resave a file on disk, choose File, Save. The document
on disk will be updated to reflect the editing changes
made to the document.

As you're typing or editing a document, resave that file
on disk frequently (every ten minutes or so) to avoid
losing hours of work to a power failure. (Although there
is a Timed Document Backup option in WordPerfect, it
should not be regarded as a substitute for saving your
documents. See BACKUP in the "Features and
Commands" section.) Be sure to save the file again when
the document is complete and before you clear the
screen or exit WordPerfect. See CLOSE and EXIT in the
"Features and Commands" secton for methods to exit a
document and clear the screen.

Once you have stored a document on disk, make a
second copy of that file on a separate disk. That way,
hard disk users will be protected if a hard disk is
accidentally formatted or "crashes," meaning that all

documents on the disk are either erased or not available
due to mechanical failure of the drive. Similarly, floppy
disk users will be protected if a floppy disk is misplaced,
ruined, or loses documents due to a mechanical
malfunction.

Managing Document Windows

WordPerfect 6.0 allows you to work with up to nine
documents simultaneously onscreen, if you have
sufficient memory in your computer to support them.
Each document is placed in a separate document window
that can be moved, resized, minimized, or maximized
with a mouse or with the keyboard.

If you are working with more than one document, you
can organize the open documents in a cascaded fashion
so that the title bar of each document is visible, or in a
tiled fashion so that the screen is divided among the
open documents. See WINDOWS in the "Features and
Commands" section for more information on managing
document windows.

You can create another document while the first one is
still in the active document window. Choose File, New.
The new document will be placed in a document
window. It will be titled "Document #" (where #
represents the number of the document window in which
the new file is located), until you save it to a disk with a
name. Moreover, if you open a document by choosing
File, Open while the first document window is occupied,
the new document will be placed in a new document
window.

PRINTING

There are two general categories of printing: from screen
or from disk. Printing from screen means that
WordPerfect prints out the version of a document
displayed in the active document window. Printing from
disk means that WordPerfect prints the version of a

document stored on disk, regardless of what is on the screen. You can choose File, Print or press SHIFT+F7 to access the print commands.

If you print a document and the document's format is incorrect, the culprit could be a hidden code you inserted accidentally. Use the Reveal Codes feature to see how your document has been formatted and to uncover and correct the problem.

If you try to print a document but the printer doesn't respond, check the Printer Control menu. (See CONTROL PRINTER in the "Features and Commands" section.) Information under the headings "Status," "Message," and "Action" often indicate the problem, which may be a simple case of the printer not being turned on. Other conditions that may prevent a document from printing include defective cables, the printer cable being attached to the wrong port on your computer, an incorrect printer driver selection in WordPerfect, a printer switch box set to the wrong device, or hardware failure.

MASTERING WORDPERFECT

WordPerfect offers a wide range of features. These can help you perform any word processing task. If what you are typing is tedious or repetitious, there is probably a WordPerfect feature that can help you out. For instance, use the Tables feature to neatly align text in columns and rows. Use the Borders feature to insert lines around the edges of each page. Use the Merge feature to personalize letters and envelopes for mass mailings. Use the Macros feature to bundle a set of repetitive keystrokes together that can be played back at your command.

In the next section, you will find features listed alphabetically. Look up and learn about any feature that can help you be more productive.

Features and Commands

The following is an alphabetical list of WordPerfect features. Each entry includes the name of the feature, the command sequence that executes it, and an explanation of that feature's purpose and applications. When you can't find what you're looking for in the alphabetical list, be sure to check the index at the back of this book for a cross-reference.

For those features where you are instructed to select one from a number of items, you can highlight the item and choose Select. An alternative for selecting with the mouse is to double-click the item.

Once you activate a feature, you must usually choose OK to return to the document onscreen. Sometimes, you must choose Close or press F7 (which acts like an exit key) to do so.

ADVANCE

Setting Horizontal Position

Choose Layout, Other (or SHIFT+F8)
Advance
Left from Cursor, Right from Cursor, or From Left Edge of
    Page

Directs the printer to advance to a specific horizontal position on the page. This is useful for filling out preprinted forms, positioning text for desktop publishing applications, typing statistical equations, or printing two sections of text in the same horizontal location.

For the Left from Cursor or Right from Cursor menu items, enter a specific measurement to move left or right from the current cursor position. For the From Left Edge of Page menu item, enter an exact horizontal measurement from the left edge of the page. In text mode, the text onscreen is not affected, but the position indicator ("Pos") on the status line indicates the horizontal location where the text will be printed.

Setting Vertical Position

Choose Layout, Other (or SHIFT+F8)
Advance
Up from Cursor, Down from Cursor, or From Top of Page

Directs the printer to advance to a specific vertical position on the page. This is useful for filling out preprinted forms, positioning text for desktop publishing applications, typing statistical equations, or printing two sections of text in the same vertical location.

For the Up from Cursor or Down from Cursor menu items, enter a specific measurement to move up or down from the current cursor position. Use the From Top of Page menu item to enter an exact vertical measurement from the top edge of the page. In text mode, the text onscreen is not affected, but the line indicator ("Ln") on the status line indicates the vertical location where the text will be printed.

ALIGNMENT CHARACTER

See DECIMAL/ALIGN CHARACTER

ALPHABETIZE TEXT

See SORT AND SELECT

APPEARANCE

Choose Font (or CTRL+F8)
Normal, Bold, Underline, Double Underline,

Italics, Outline, Shadow, Small Caps,
Redline, or Strikeout

For a particular font, alters the attribute that controls the
look of characters at the printer. Appearance attributes
include Bold, Underline, Double Underline, Italics,
Outline, Shadow, Small Caps, Redline, and Strikeout. Be
aware that some printers do not support all of these
appearance attributes for a given font.

To activate an appearance attribute as you type, follow
the preceding instructions to turn on the desired
appearance attribute. (You can repeat the command
sequence and turn on as many appearance attributes as
desired.) Next, type the text, and then turn off the
appearance attribute by either 1) pressing the right
arrow key to move the cursor off of the end attribute
code, 2) repeating the same command sequence as when
you turned on the attribute, or 3) choosing Font, Normal
(or pressing CTRL+N) to turn off all attributes if more than
one is active.

To activate an appearance attribute for existing text, use
the Block feature to highlight the existing text before
following the preceding instructions.

Onscreen, the text controlled by a given appearance
attribute displays in a different color or brightness to
distinguish it from normal text when working in text
mode (see COLORS ON SCREEN). In graphics and page
modes, the onscreen effect of appearance attributes will
attempt to match the printed document.

See also the separate entries for attributes for which
other command sequences are available: BOLD, ITALICS,
and UNDERLINE. For redline and strikeout, see also
REDLINE, DOCUMENT COMPARE, STRIKEOUT, and
REMOVE REDLINE AND STRIKEOUT.

APPEND

Blocking Text

Block the text
Choose Edit, Append (or CTRL+F4)
To File or Clipboard

Attaches the highlighted text to the end of a file
currently on disk, or to the currently active Shell
Clipboard (if you loaded WordPerfect from Shell.) To
append to a file, type in the name of an existing file and
press ENTER. If the filename you enter cannot be found,
the file is created for you by WordPerfect.

Blocking a Sentence, Paragraph, or Page

Position cursor within the sentence, paragraph, or page
Choose Edit, Select (or CTRL+F4)
Sentence, Paragraph, or Page
Edit, Append
To File or Clipboard

Attaches the highlighted sentence, paragraph, or page to
the end of a file currently on disk or to the currently
active Shell Clipboard.

ASCII FILES

See SAVE AS

ATTRIBUTE CHANGE

See APPEARANCE and SIZE/POSITION for a change on the printed page; *see* COLORS ON SCREEN for a change onscreen

AUTO CODE PLACEMENT

Choose File, Setup (or SHIFT+F1)
Environment
Auto Code Placement

Enabled by default (a checkmark appears in the checkbox). When codes affecting page and paragraph layout are inserted in a document, they are automatically placed at the appropriate locations. Codes specific to page layout are placed at the beginning of the page the cursor is located on. Codes specific to paragraph layout are inserted at the beginning of the paragraph where the cursor is located.

When this feature is disabled, codes are inserted at the cursor location.

Certain codes, such as appearance attribute codes (bold, underline, and so on) are not affected by the Auto Code Placement feature.

BACK TAB

Layout, Alignment, Back Tab (or SHIFT+TAB)

Used to move the cursor and any subsequent text to the previous tab location. If tab locations exist to the left of the left margin, Back Tab can also be used as a margin release.

BACKUP

Drive/Directory Location

Determines where timed backup files are stored on disk (see LOCATION OF FILES).

Safeguarding Original

File, Setup (or SHIFT+F1)
Environment
Backup Options
Back Up Original Document (.BK!) on Save or Exit

Safeguards against accidentally replacing an original file on disk with the document on your screen. As you edit a document onscreen and resave it using the same filename, WordPerfect prompts "Replace?"; if you press Y to replace, the document onscreen is saved under the same filename, while the original document on disk is renamed with the same filename but with the .BK! extension.

This feature is turned off by default. Selecting the item in the Backup dialog box (placing a checkmark in the box to the left of its name) will enable the feature. If you turn the feature on and then inadvertently replace an original file, you can retrieve and rename the file with the .BK! extension.

Setting Timed Backup

Choose File, Setup (or SHIFT+F1)
Environment
Backup Options
Timed Document Backup

Safeguards against the loss of text from the document onscreen in the case of a power or machine failure. Text in the active document window is stored at the time interval specified in a file named WP{WPC}.BK#, where # represents the number of the document window (1-9).

To select the Timed Backup feature, make sure there is an X in the checkbox next to the name of the feature. You must also enter a time interval representing the number of minutes between each backup (the default is ten minutes). If you turn the feature on and experience a power or machine failure, restart WordPerfect. Then you are given the choice to open, rename, or delete the backup file(s).

BALANCED COLUMNS

See TEXT COLUMNS

BAR CODES

Choose Layout (or SHIFT+F8)
Other, Bar Code
Type 5-, 9- or 11-digit zip code

Creates a series of long and short lines from a zip code. Speeds mail sorting at the post office. Useful next to addresses that will appear in the window of an envelope. See also ENVELOPES for the procedure to insert bar codes on envelopes.

BASELINE PLACEMENT FOR TYPESETTERS

Layout, Document (or SHIFT+F8)
Baseline Placement for Typesetters

Allows you to set the baseline (the bottom of the first line of text) even with the top margin. This ensures that the baseline will remain constant despite possible font changes in the text. Normally, the top of the first line of text is placed even with the top margin, so that the baseline is somewhat below the top margin. Baseline Placement has an effect only if you previously set Line Height to a fixed measurement (see LINE HEIGHT).

BEEP OPTIONS

File, Setup (or SHIFT+F1)
Environment
Beep Options
Beep on Error, Beep on Hyphenation, or Beep on Search
  Failure

Determines whether or not the computer sounds a beep in three distinct situations: 1) when an error message appears on the status line, 2) when a request for a hyphenation decision appears on the status line, or 3) when a "*Not Found*" message appears on the status line after a search.

BINDING OFFSET

Layout (or SHIFT+F8)
Other, Printer Functions, Binding Offset
Specify the Measurement
Specify the Binding Edge

Sets an extra-wide margin for a document that you plan to bind like a book. By default, the binding offset is set from the left edge for odd-numbered pages and from the right edge for even-numbered pages.

BLOCK

Position cursor at one end of the text
Choose Edit, Block (or F12 or ALT+F4)
Position cursor at the opposite end of the text

Marks off (highlights) a portion of a document on which commands can be performed. The cursor must be on the first or after the last character in the text before you press BLOCK. When you press BLOCK, the message "Block on" appears on the screen. You can then use the cursor movement keys or the Search feature to move the cursor to the opposite end of the block. Or, if you are moving the cursor forward, you also can type a character to move to that character. The text in the block becomes highlighted in reverse video. (See also MOUSE and SELECT for additional methods for blocking text.)

Block text whenever you wish to limit a command to that section. For instance, block a section of text and then issue the Print command. Or, block a section of text and then change the font or font attribute. Or, block a section of text and then change the layout.

BLOCK PROTECT

Block the text
Choose Layout (or SHIFT+F8)
Other, Block Protect

Ensures that a block of text is not divided by a soft page break. This is useful to keep all lines of a table or chart on the same page. It is inserted automatically when typing in parallel columns with block protection to keep the parallel columns together and safe from a page break.

BOLD

Produces characters that are boldface (darker than normal) when printed. In text mode, the bold text will be displayed on the screen in a different color or brightness to distinguish it from normal text. (See also COLORS ON SCREEN to set the way that the bold attribute is displayed onscreen.) In graphics or page layout modes, the text will appear darker.

For Existing Text

Block the text
Choose F<u>o</u>nt, <u>B</u>old (or F6 or CTRL+B)

The Bold attribute will be applied only to the text in the block.

For Text About to Be Typed

F<u>o</u>nt, <u>B</u>old (or F6 or CTRL+B) to turn on bold
Type the text
F<u>o</u>nt, <u>B</u>old (or F6 or CTRL+B) to turn off bold

When you turn off the Bold feature, the cursor is moved to the right of the "Bold Off" code. In addition to using the menu commands or pressing F6 or CTRL+B, you can also tap the RIGHT ARROW key.

BOOKLETS

See SUBDIVIDE PAGE

BOOKMARK

Holds a place in a document, allowing you to return to that location quickly. You can create named bookmarks or

use a generic bookmark, called a *Quickmark*. You can
have as many bookmarks as you like, but you can only
use one Quickmark in each document. WordPerfect
automatically places the Quickmark at the cursor location
when you save a file so that you can quickly return to
that location when you reopen the document.

Creating a Bookmark

Place the cursor in the desired location for the bookmark
Choose Edit, Bookmark (or SHIFT+F12)
Create
Type the name of the bookmark

Finding a Bookmark

Choose Edit, Bookmark (or SHIFT+F12)
Highlight the desired bookmark in the list
Find

Creating a Quickmark

Place the cursor in the desired location for the Quickmark
Choose Edit, Bookmark (or SHIFT+F12)
Set Quickmark

A shortcut for Edit, Bookmark, Set Quickmark is CTRL+Q.

Finding a Quickmark

Choose Edit, Bookmark (or SHIFT+F12)
Find Quickmark

A shortcut for Edit, Bookmark, Find Quickmark is CTRL+F.

BORDERS

Used to create graphical lines around paragraphs, pages,
or text columns. Also used around other graphics
elements, such as tables and graphics boxes.

Choosing Predefined Border Styles

Position the cursor within the paragraph, page or column
Choose Graphics (or ALT+F9)
Borders
Paragraph, Page, or Column
Border Style
Select a predefined border style

Once a border style is selected, you can add fill (shading) to a border by choosing Fill. (See FILL STYLES.) Or, you can customize the border by choosing Customize and then modifying lines, color, spacing, shadow, corners, or fill as desired.

After a border style has been added to a document, it remains in effect until you turn it off. In other words, if you place a border around a paragraph, as you type subsequent paragraphs, the border will expand to include them. If this is not the result you desire, you must turn off the feature to keep from surrounding the subsequent paragraphs with a border. Repeat the steps above and choose Off. Another alternative is to block text before you apply a border.

Modifying Border Styles

Choose Graphics (or ALT+F9)
Borders, Styles

Lets you create or edit a border style for all graphics elements that use that style. You can also modify a border style if you choose Based on Border Style while customizing the style.

BOXES

See GRAPHICS BOXES

BULLETS

Places bullet characters (small circles, either hollow or filled) in the text. There are several methods for inserting a bullet. You can use the Special Characters feature to insert a bullet from the typographical symbols character set. (See SPECIAL CHARACTERS.) Or, if you know the character number of the bullet you want to insert, use the Compose feature. (See COMPOSE.) You can insert bullets as part of an outline. (See OUTLINING.)

Moreover, you can use the Bullet Coach to insert bullets in your document. The Coach offers you a predefined group of characters that are suitable for bullets. To run the Bullet Coach, choose Help, Coaches, position the cursor on Bullet Coach, and choose OK; then follow the instructions on the screen.

BUTTON BAR

Gives you easy access to frequently used commands. A bar containing buttons appears onscreen. Each button represents a different command. You must have a mouse to use a Button Bar.

There are seven predefined Button Bars that can be made visible from the document window, and it is possible to create customized Button Bars. There are also Button Bars that are visible from the Print Preview screen, the Image Editor, and the Equations Editor.

Creating a New Button Bar

Choose View, Button Bar Setup, Select, Create
Enter the name of the new Button Bar
Add Menu Item, Add Feature, Add Macro or Add Button Bar

If you are adding a menu item, the menu bar is activated so that you can choose commands. When you are finished selecting menu items, press the F7 key.

If you are adding a feature, macro, or Button Bar, you will be presented with a list box. Choose the desired item from the list box, then choose Select. When you are finished selecting from the list box, choose OK.

Editing a Button Bar

Choose View, Button Bar Setup, Edit

WordPerfect assumes that you wish to edit the currently active Button Bar. If that is not the case, first follow the instructions above under "Selecting a Button Bar" to select the Button Bar to be edited.

To add a menu item, feature, macro, or Button Bar, follow the instructions above in "Creating a Button Bar."

To delete a button, highlight the name of the button you wish to delete. Choose Delete Button. You will be presented with a dialog box asking you to confirm the deletion. Choose Yes to delete or No to cancel the deletion.

To move a button, highlight the name of the button you wish to move. Choose Move Button. (Notice that the Move option now becomes a Paste option.) Next, highlight the name of the button above which you wish to place the button being moved. Choose Paste Button.

Hiding/Displaying the Button Bar

Choose View, Button Bar

Your choice to display or hide a Button Bar has an effect in text mode independent from graphics or page mode.

Modifying Button Bar Options

Choose View, Button Bar Setup, Options
Mark the desired Position and Style options

Determines the location of the Button Bar onscreen and whether the bar contains text, pictures, or both.

Selecting a Different Button Bar

Choose View, Button Bar Setup, Select
Highlight the desired Button Bar
Select

CALCULATE

See MATH COLUMNS and TABLES

CANCEL

ESC

Has various functions depending on the status of the screen: clears a menu, dialog box, or prompt from the screen; stops a macro or merge if one is in process; activates the Undelete feature (see UNDELETE).

You can also cancel a command with a mouse by clicking the middle mouse button on a three-button mouse or by clicking the left and right mouse buttons simultaneously on a two-button mouse.

CANCEL A PRINT JOB

See CONTROL PRINTER

CAPITALIZATION

CAPS LOCK

Produces characters that are all uppercase onscreen and when printed. CAPS LOCK affects only the letters A to Z.

To activate capitalization as you type, press CAPS LOCK, type the text, and then press CAPS LOCK a second time to turn off capitalization. (The CAPS LOCK key is a toggle switch; it turns capitalization on if it was off and vice versa.) When CAPS LOCK is activated, the letters you type while pressing SHIFT appear in lowercase rather than uppercase. (To activate capitalization for existing text, see CASE CONVERSION.)

CAPTIONS

See GRAPHICS BOXES

CARTRIDGES/FONTS/PRINTWHEELS

Choose File, Print (or SHIFT+F7)
Select
Position cursor on a printer name
Edit
Select Cartridges/Fonts/Print Wheels
Position cursor on font category of your choice
Choose OK
Position cursor on font or cartridge name
* Present when job begins or
   + Can be loaded/unloaded during job

Defines additional cartridges, soft fonts, or print wheels that you have available for use with your printer.

Cartridges and built-in fonts can only be marked with an asterisk (*) because they must always be present when the print job begins. Your cartridge selections cannot exceed the number of cartridge slots available in the printer. Look in the "Quantity" box to determine how many cartridge selections can be made.

Soft fonts can be marked with either an asterisk (*) or a plus symbol (+). Marking with the plus symbol provides the most flexibility because WordPerfect then controls whether fonts are loaded or unloaded to and from the printer's memory during a print job. If you mark soft fonts with an asterisk, you will have to initialize the printer every time a new print job requires a different set of fonts. Marking soft fonts with a plus symbol makes it unnecessary to initialize the printer.

The soft fonts and the fonts on the cartridges and print wheels that you marked will now appear on the Font menu (see FONT).

CASCADING WINDOWS

See WINDOWS

CASE CONVERSION

Block the text
Choose Edit, Convert Case (or SHIFT+F3)
Uppercase, Lowercase, or Initial Caps

Switches a highlighted block of text to all uppercase, all lowercase, or initial cap letters. When you switch to lowercase, the first character of a sentence remains in uppercase if the punctuation from the preceding sentence is included in the highlighted block. Also, the personal pronoun "I" is always capitalized, as are words beginning with "I" followed by an apostrophe. When you use Initial Caps, words such as *a, an, and,* and *the* are not capitalized.

CENTER

Choose Layout, Alignment, Center (or SHIFT+F6)
Type text
Press ENTER to end centering

Centers a short line of text between the left and right margins. (If you press TAB to tab over to a tab stop and then choose center alignment, text is centered on the tab stop.)

To center existing text, position the cursor on the first character, choose center alignment, and then press the down arrow key. If you first use the Block feature to highlight a section of text and then choose center alignment, numerous lines can be centered all at once (see also JUSTIFICATION).

Choose center alignment twice in a row to precede text with dot leaders (....).

CENTER PAGE TOP TO BOTTOM

Position cursor on page where vertical
    centering should begin
Choose Layout, Page
Center Current Page or Center Pages

Centers text vertically between the top and bottom margins. Useful to center the text of a title page or a short letter.

Choose Center Current Page to activate vertical centering for the current page only. Choose Center Pages to activate vertical centering for the current and succeeding pages. To turn off vertical centering, place the cursor on the page where vertical centering should be disabled. Then follow the steps above, but remove the checkmark from the option to be disabled.

CHANGE DRIVE/DIRECTORY

See DEFAULT DRIVE/DIRECTORY, CHANGE

CLIPBOARD

See SHELL, EXIT TO

CLOSE DOCUMENT

Choose File, Close

Clears the document currently onscreen and closes the document window. (However, when only one document window is open, the window remains open.)

If the document onscreen has been modified since it was last saved (or has never been saved), then before the document is cleared from the screen, a dialog box appears with four options: Save As lets you specify a new filename to save the document on disk. Yes saves the document using the old filename (assuming the document has previously been saved); the document on disk will be updated with the modifications in the document window. No closes the document window without saving the document. Cancel returns you to the document, aborting the Close command.

You can also close a document and document window using the Exit command. (See EXIT DOCUMENT.)

COACHES

See HELP

CODE PAGE

Choose File, Save As
Type a name for the file

Choose Code Page (or F9)
Highlight the desired Code Page
Choose Select

A Code Page defines the ASCII character set that is used in a document. Different Code Pages are used for different languages. You can change the Code Page when you save a document.

CODES

See REVEAL CODES

COLORS AT THE PRINTER

Choose Font (or CTRL+F8)
Print Color
Highlight the desired color
Select

Providing that you have a color printer, sets the color for text on the printed page. Seventy colors are predefined (not all may be available with your printer). You can vary the shade of the color you choose by choosing Shade and typing in the percentage of density. You can also design your own custom colors by entering a new intensity percentage for red, green, and blue.

To cancel the Print Color feature later in the text, reposition the cursor and repeat the same command sequence, except choose Black as the new color. You can also change the Print Color for blocked text.

The color in which the text prints is independent of the onscreen color of text (see COLORS ON SCREEN to set the onscreen color of text).

COLORS ON SCREEN

Lets you choose a screen type and color scheme for your
monitor. It also allows you to edit or create a color
scheme to control the way screen elements are displayed
in the document window. The options available to you,
and thus the procedures for setting the onscreen display,
depend on your display card and monitor.

Changing the Color Scheme

Choose File, Setup (or SHIFT+F1)
Display
Graphics Mode Screen Type/Colors or Text Mode Screen
              Type/Colors
Color Schemes

Position the cursor on the color scheme that you want
and choose Select.

Changing the Screen Type

Choose File, Setup (or SHIFT+F1)
Display
Graphics Mode Screen Type/Colors or Text Mode Screen
              Type/Colors
Screen Type

In the Screen Type dialog box, highlight the name of the
driver that matches your monitor and card, then choose
Select. Make sure you are in graphics mode to change
the graphics mode screen type, and Text mode to change
the text mode screen type.

Editing the Graphics Mode Color Scheme

Choose File, Setup (or SHIFT+F1)
Display
Graphics Mode Screen Type/Colors
Color Schemes

Highlight the color scheme you wish to edit
Edit
Screen Elements
Highlight the screen element you wish to affect
Color

You cannot change the default color schemes. Instead,
copy the color scheme to another name, then edit the
copied color scheme.

Editing the Text Mode Color Scheme

Choose File, Setup (or SHIFT+F1)
Display
Text Mode Screen Type/Colors
Highlight the desired color scheme
Edit
Text Attributes or Menus & Dialogs
Attributes
Highlight the Attribute you wish to affect
Color or Font
Highlight the desired color or attribute

You cannot change the default color schemes. Instead,
copy the color scheme to another name, then edit the
copied color scheme.

COLUMNS

See MATH COLUMNS, TABS, and TEXT COLUMNS

COMMENTS

Converting to Text

Position cursor below the comment
Choose Layout (or CTRL+F7)
Comment, Convert to Text

Transforms the content of a comment into regular text so that it can be edited and printed as part of the document.

Converting Text to a Comment

Block the text to be converted
Choose Layout (or CTRL+F7)
Comment, Create

Creating Comments

Choose Layout (or CTRL+F7)
Comment, Create
Type the text to be included in the comment
Press F7

Creates a document comment in a double-line box, which is displayed on the screen but is not printed. A comment is useful when you wish to insert a reminder for yourself or someone else who will work with that document. (To delete the comment, delete the code that is inserted on the Reveal Codes screen.)

Displaying Comments

Choose View, Screen Setup
Window Options, Display Comments

Specifies whether you wish to display all comments onscreen or to hide them from view. Place a checkmark in the Display Comments checkbox to display document comments, or remove the checkmark to hide the display of comments onscreen.

Editing Comments

Position the cursor below the comment
Choose Layout (or CTRL+F7)
Comment, Edit
Make the desired changes
Press F7

Edits the contents of a comment. WordPerfect first searches backwards to find the comment, so if your document contains more than one comment, position the cursor below the comment you wish to edit.

COMPARE DOCUMENTS

See DOCUMENT COMPARE

COMPOSE

CTRL+A
Type the characters to be combined or
   the WordPerfect Character Set Number

Allows you to insert a *digraph,* which is two vowels or consonants combined to express one sound (such as æ), or a *diacritical mark,* which is a vowel or consonant combined with a symbol to express one sound (such as ñ). Type the two symbols that make up the digraph or diacritical mark. For instance, after typing CTRL+A, type ~n to insert ñ.

You can also insert a special character if you know its WordPerfect Character number. For instance, after typing CTRL+A, type 4,6 to insert the section symbol into your document onscreen.

Be aware that certain monitors cannot display specific special characters, and certain non-graphics printers cannot print specific special characters. (For more on special characters, see SPECIAL CHARACTERS.)

CONCORDANCE

See INDEXES

CONDITIONAL END OF PAGE

Position cursor above first line to be included
Choose Layout (or SHIFT+F8)
Other, Conditional End of Page

Ensures that a group of lines remains undivided by a soft page break. This is useful to keep a heading together with its accompanying text.

Position the cursor on the line before the text you wish to keep together before starting the command sequence. In the box next to "Number of Lines to Keep Together:", type in the number of lines and press ENTER, then choose OK. Beginning with the next line, the specified number of lines will stay on the same page. (For other ways to control page breaks, see also BLOCK PROTECT, PAGE BREAKS, and WIDOW/ORPHAN PROTECTION.)

CONTROL PRINTER

Choose File, Print (or SHIFT+F7)
Control Printer
Cancel Job, Rush Job, * (Un)Mark, or (Un)Mark All

Manages print jobs. The Current Job box contains information about the currently active print job. If a problem occurs during the print job, a message will be displayed here along with suggestions for resolving the problem. The following features can be used to manage both active jobs and jobs in the print queue:

- Cancel Job: Removes one or all print jobs from the print queue. (If any part of a print job has already been sent to the printer's buffer, WordPerfect will not be able to control that portion of the job. If you cancel the job, the portion that is being controlled by the printer's buffer will continue to print.)

- Rush Job: Rearranges the order of print jobs in the print queue, moving a specified job to the top of the list.

- Display Jobs: Displays all print jobs, which is useful if there are more print jobs than can be displayed on the Control Printer Screen.

- Go (start printer): Resumes printing after a pause to insert a new print wheel, to manually feed paper, or after stopping a print job.

- Stop: Stops the printer (without removing a job from the print queue) until you choose Go to resume printing or Cancel to cancel the print job.

- Network: Displays a list of jobs that have been sent to the network printing queue.

CONVERT FILES TO/FROM WORDPERFECT

Converts to and from WordPerfect format. These methods only allow you to work with one file at a time. (To convert a group of documents at one time, see CONVERTPERFECT.)

Converting Files Created in Other Formats

Choose File, Open (or SHIFT+F10)
Type the name of the file
Choose OK
Highlight the format in the File Format dialog box
Choose Select

WordPerfect will try to discern the file's original format and will place the cursor on the name of the format it believes is correct in the File Format dialog box. When you choose Select, the file will be retrieved to the document window in WordPerfect 6.0 format. (It is not necessary to convert documents created with

WordPerfect 5.1/5.2. The conversion will occur automatically when you open the files.)

Fifty-five formats can be converted through the Open File dialog box. Supported file formats include the 48 listed in "Saving Files in Another Format," plus Lotus 1-2-3 versions 2.3-3.1 and PlanPerfect 3.0-5.1.

Saving Files in Other Formats

Choose File, Save As
Type the name of the file
Format
Highlight the desired format

WordPerfect 6.0 files can be saved in 48 other formats including Ami Pro 1.2-3.0 (Windows), ASCII Standard and Stripped, DisplayWrite 4.0-5.0, DOS Delimited Text, IBM DCA FFT and RFT, Kermit, MS Word 4.0-5.5, MS Word for Windows 1.0-2.0b, MultiMate 3.3-4.0, MultiMate Advantage 3.6, Multimate Advantage II 1.0, Navy DIF, OfficeWriter 6.0-6.2, Quattro Pro 3.0-4.0, Rich Text Format (RTF), Spreadsheet DIF, WordPerfect 4.2, WordStar 2000 1.0-3.0, and WordStar 3.3-6.0.

CONVERTPERFECT

Exit WordPerfect to DOS
Type **CV** [Source File] [Target File] [Target Format]

Executes the CV.EXE file, which is stored on your hard disk in the WordPerfect program directory. This file transfers files from 73 formats into WordPerfect version 6.0 format and vice versa.

COPY

Block text to be copied
Choose Edit, Copy (or CTRL+C)

Move cursor to the location for the copied text
Edit, Paste (or CTRL+V)

Performs a copy in two separate keystrokes. An
additional copy of the text will be created in the
specified location. The original text will be unaffected by
this editing maneuver. See also DRAG AND DROP for a
way to copy using a mouse.

COPY FILES

Choose File, File Manager (or F5)
Type drive or directory name and press ENTER
Position cursor on a file
Copy
Type drive or directory name and press ENTER

Places a second copy of the file into a new drive or
directory. This is useful when you wish to back up files
as a safety precaution, or if you wish to reorganize files
on disk.

You can copy two or more files in one command by
marking the files you wish to copy with an asterisk
before selecting Copy (see MARK FILES).

COPY AND PASTE

Block text to be copied
Choose Edit, Copy and Paste (or CTRL+INS)
Move cursor to the location for the copied text
Press ENTER

Performs a copy in back-to-back keystrokes. This
technique assumes that the copy should be pasted in
another location as part of the same operation. After
choosing Copy and Paste from the Edit menu, the prompt
"Move cursor; press ENTER to Retrieve" appears on the
status line. The copied text will be placed at the cursor

location when the ENTER key is pressed. The original text will be unaffected by this editing maneuver. See also DRAG AND DROP, for a way to copy using a mouse, and SELECT, to copy and paste tabular columns and rectangles.

CROSS-REFERENCE

Marking References and Targets

Position cursor in the referring text
Choose Tools (or ALT+F5)
Cross-Reference, Both
Tie Reference to
Choose Page, Secondary Page, Chapter, Volume,
    Paragraph/Outline, Footnote, Endnote,
    Chapter Number, or Counter
Target Name
Type name for the target text
Choose OK
Position cursor in location immediately following
    target and press ENTER

Creates a reference to a specific location in the document. For example, the reference may be "Refer to page 44", where the target is page 44. The reference and target are marked in the same operation.

Under "Target Name" in the Mark Cross-Reference and Target dialog box, indicate a name that ties the reference and target. The reference code (and thus the position of the cursor when you begin the operation) can be placed in regular text, a header, a footer, a footnote, or an endnote. A target code can be placed in regular text on a page, next to a paragraph/outline number, in a footnote or endnote, or in a graphics box caption.

Marking References Only

Position cursor in the referring text
Choose Tools (or ALT+F5)
Cross-Reference, Reference
Tie Reference to
Choose Page, Secondary Page, Chapter, Volume,
   Paragraph/Outline, Footnote, Endnote,
   Chapter Number, or Counter
Target Name
Type name for the target text
Choose OK
Position cursor in location immediately following
   reference
Press ENTER

Useful if you wish to mark the reference and target separately or if you wish to create multiple references to the same target. A question mark appears in place of the reference number, such as "Refer to Page ?". After you mark the target in a separate operation, you must then update the cross-reference (see "Update").

Under "Target Name" in the Mark Cross-Reference dialog box, indicate a name that ties the reference and target. The reference code (and thus the position of the cursor when you begin the operation) can be placed in regular text, a header, a footer, a footnote, or an endnote. A target code can be placed in regular text on a page, next to a paragraph/outline number, in a footnote or endnote, or in a graphics box caption.

Marking Targets Only

Position cursor in location immediately following target
Choose Tools (or ALT+F5)
Cross Reference, Target
Type target name

Useful if you wish to mark the reference and target separately or if you wish to create multiple targets for a single reference. After you mark the target in a separate operation, you must then update the cross-reference (see "Update").

When typing a target name in the Mark Cross-Reference Target dialog box, indicate a name that has also been used for the reference. A target code can be placed in regular text on a page, next to a paragraph/outline number, in a footnote or endnote, or in a graphics box caption.

Updating Cross-References

Updates the cross-references in a document, which is necessary if you either marked the reference and target separately, or edited the text after marking the references and targets, so that the references must be revised. (See GENERATE CROSS-REFERENCES, INDEXES, LISTS, AND TABLES for the key sequence.)

CURSOR MOVEMENT KEYS

See the "General Reminders" section at the beginning of the book

CURSOR SPEED

Choose File, Setup (or SHIFT+F1)
Environment, Cursor Speed

Increases or decreases the speed with which keys repeat on the keyboard when they are held down. By default, WordPerfect is set to repeat 50 times for every second a key is held down. Other options include 15, 20, 30, or 40 characters per second, as well as Normal, which returns your keyboard to its normal cursor speed and avoids potential incompatibilities with terminate-and-stay-resident (TSR) programs.

CUT (FOR A MOVE)

Block text to be cut
Choose Edit, Cut (or CTRL+X)
Move cursor to the location for the cut text
Edit, Paste (or CTRL+V)

Performs a move in two separate keystrokes. Removes
the blocked text from the document. Cut text is held
temporarily in memory (until it is replaced by other cut or
copied text) and can be retrieved to a new location in the
current document or another document with the Paste
command. See also DRAG AND DROP for a way to move
using a mouse.

CUT AND PASTE

Block the text to be cut and pasted
Choose Edit, Cut and Paste (or CTRL+DEL)
Move cursor to new location for the cut text
Press ENTER

Performs a move in back-to-back keystrokes. Assumes
that cut text will immediately be pasted into another
location in the current document or another document.
After choosing Cut and Paste, the prompt "Move cursor;
press ENTER to Retrieve" appears on the status line.
Move the cursor to the new location for the cut text and
press the ENTER key. The cut text will be pasted into the
new location. See also DRAG AND DROP, for a way to
move using a mouse, and SELECT, to cut and paste
tabular columns and rectangles.

DATE (AND TIME)

Inserting as Code

Place cursor in text where date should be inserted
Choose Tools, Date (or SHIFT+F5)
Code

Inserts the date and/or time onscreen as a hidden code in
the current date format. The date or time will be updated
whenever you retrieve or print that document. To use
this feature correctly, be sure that the computer's clock
has been set.

Inserting as Text

Choose Tools, Date (or SHIFT+F5)
Text

Inserts the date and/or time on the screen as text, using
the current date format. To use this feature correctly, be
sure that the computer's clock has been set.

Setting a Format

Choose Tools, Date (or SHIFT+F5)
Format

Specifies the way the date and/or time are displayed
when you insert the date (either as text or as a code)
using the Date feature on the Tools menu. Eight
predefined formats are available. Customized date and
time formats including text, numbers, and punctuation
can be created by choosing Edit in the Date Formats
dialog box. This format stays in effect for the entire
working session or until you again change the date
format. The default date format is Month ##, 19##, which
can be permanently altered in Initial Codes Setup (see
INITIAL SETTINGS).

DECIMAL/ALIGN CHARACTER

Choose Layout (or SHIFT+F8)
Character, Decimal/Align Character

Alters the character used with the Tab Align, Tabs, and
Math features to align numbers (see also TAB ALIGN,
TABS, and MATH COLUMNS). The default is the period.

DEFAULT DRIVE/DIRECTORY, CHANGE

Choose File, File Manager (or F5)
=
Enter drive and/or directory name

or

Choose File, File Manager (or F5)
Choose OK
Change directory
Enter drive or directory name

Changes the default for where WordPerfect assumes you
wish to save files to and retrieve files from for the entire
working session, or until you change the default again.
Indicate a specific disk drive by typing the appropriate
drive letter followed by a colon, such as A:, B:, or C:.
Indicate a directory on the hard disk (C:) by preceding
each directory level with a backslash, as in C:\WPDOCS,
C:\WPDOCS\DATA, or C:\WPDOCS\BUD. (See also
LOCATION OF FILES for the procedure to establish the
same default drive/directory at the start of each working
session.)

DEFAULT SETTINGS, CHANGE

See INITIAL SETTINGS

DELAY CODES

Choose Layout (or SHIFT+F8)
Page, Delay Codes
Type number of pages to be delayed
Choose OK
Enter code(s) to be delayed
Press F7

Delays any open code (for example, font, line spacing, justification) for a specified number of pages after the current page. The delay code will be placed either at the top of the document or after the most recent hard page break.

DELETE CODES

Choose View, Reveal Codes
Locate the code to be deleted
DEL or BACKSPACE

Erases a code from the screen, thus aborting the effect of a feature that was activated by initially inserting that code. Locate a code that you wish to delete using either the Reveal Codes or Search feature (see these separate entries), and then delete the code using the DEL or BACKSPACE key. The Reveal Codes screen must be displayed in order to delete a code from a document. If you delete one code of a pair, the other code is automatically deleted.

You can also use the Macro or Replace feature (see MACROS and REPLACE) to delete all occurrences of a given code in a document.

DELETE FILES

Choose File, File Manager (or F5)
Type drive or directory name and press ENTER
Position cursor on file
Delete, Yes to confirm

Deletes a file from disk, which is useful when the file is obsolete and you wish to free up space on disk.

You can delete two or more files in one command by marking the files you wish to delete with an asterisk before selecting Delete (see MARK FILES).

DELETE TEXT

Lets you remove text from your document. Refer to UNDELETE for how to restore text that you delete accidentally.

Blocking Text

Block the text
DEL or BACKSPACE

Deletes the block. Another alternative is to delete a block that is a tabular column or rectangle.

To delete a tabular column, which is text or numbers aligned on a tab stop, position the cursor on any character in the first line of the column, choose Edit, Block (or F12 or ALT+F4), and then position the cursor on any character in the last line of the column. Then choose Edit, Select, Tabular Column, Delete.

To delete a rectangle, position the cursor on the character that represents the upper-left corner of the rectangle, choose Edit, Block (or F12 or ALT+F4), and then use the cursor to highlight up to the character that represents the lower-right corner of the rectangle. Then choose Edit, Select, Rectangle, Delete.

Blocking Character(s), Word(s), and Line(s)

See the "General Reminders" section

Blocking a Sentence, Paragraph, or Page

Position cursor within the sentence, paragraph, or page
Choose Edit, Select
Sentence, Paragraph, or Page
Choose Delete

Deletes the highlighted sentence, paragraph, or page.

DESCRIPTIVE NAME

Setting Up the Descriptive Type Feature

Choose File, File Manager (or F5)
Enter the desired directory name
Setup (SHIFT+F1)
Display List Mode
Descriptive Names and Types

Enables you to view descriptive document names that you assigned to your files, rather than being restricted to the standard, short (8-character) filename. A descriptive name can be up to 255 characters in length, contain a filename extension of up to 255 characters, and contain spaces. At the same time, a document type can also be assigned to further describe each file.

You can indicate a descriptive name when you create a document summary for a document. See SUMMARY, DOCUMENT.

DICTIONARY

See SPELL

DIGRAPHS/DIACRITICAL MARKS

See COMPOSE

DIRECTORY

Changing the Default

See DEFAULT DRIVE/DIRECTORY, CHANGE

Creating a Directory

Choose File, File Manager (or F5)
=
Enter new directory name

or

Choose File, File Manager (or F5)
Change Directory
Type new directory name
Choose OK
Yes to confirm

Creates a new directory and is most useful for hard disk users who create directories as a way of organizing files on disk.

Deleting a Directory

Choose File, File Manager (or F5)
Type name of parent directory and press ENTER
Position cursor on name of subdirectory to be deleted
Delete
Yes to confirm

Erases a directory from disk. This can only be
accomplished when the directory contains no files or
subdirectories. Also, a list of files for the parent of the
directory you wish to delete must be displayed.

DIRECTORY TREE

Choose File, File Manager (or F5)
Directory Tree (or F8)

Allows you to select a directory that will be displayed in
the File Manager. The Directory Tree provides a
graphical illustration of the directory structure
(hierarchy) of the specified drive. You can scroll the
cursor up and down in the hierarchy. The following
options are available:

- Select Directory: Changes the display to the list so that
  you can see the contents of a directory.

- Other Drive: Displays the directory structure on a specified drive.

- Rescan Drive: Updates the tree so that you can see
  changes resulting from creating, renaming, or deleting
  directories.

- Use as Pattern: Inserts the name of the highlighted directory into the Specify File Manager list.

- Name Search: Search for a directory by typing its name.

- Search (F2): Search for a directory by typing its name.

- Print Tree (SHIFT+F7): Send the directory tree image to the printer.

DISPLAY

For information on the three display (or view modes), see the "General Reminders" section. For information on changing the screen display colors, see COLOR ON SCREEN.

DISPLAY PITCH

Choose Layout (or SHIFT+F8)
Document, Display Pitch
Type value and choose Manual or
    press ENTER and choose Automatic

Sets the amount of horizontal space that one character occupies onscreen. Decreasing the pitch expands the document horizontally. Useful for altering text onscreen when text is formatted into columns or when using tabs and indents, where text appears to overlap onscreen.

DOCUMENT COMMENTS

See COMMENTS

DOCUMENT COMPARE

Retrieve version of file to be compared
Choose File, Compare Documents (or ALT+F5)
Add Markings, Document on Disk
Type name of document to which current

document should be compared
Compare by
Word, Phrase, Sentence or Paragraph

Compares a document on the screen to a document on disk. It is useful after you have edited a contract or other document and you wish to compare the original with the revision. WordPerfect gives you the option of comparing the documents by word, phrase, sentence, or paragraph.

Onscreen text that does not exist in the file on disk is redlined. Text in the file on disk that does not exist in the document on the screen is copied to the onscreen document with strikeout codes inserted. (See also REDLINE and STRIKEOUT.) For a section of text that is moved, WordPerfect inserts "The Following Text Was Moved" before the text and "The Preceding Text Was Moved" after the text.

(See also REMOVE REDLINE AND STRIKEOUT for the method to return the onscreen document to its edited version.)

DOCUMENT FORMAT

See FORMAT

DOCUMENT INFORMATION

Choose Tools, Writing Tools
Document Information
Choose OK when finished reviewing statistics

Provides statistics concerning the current document, including the number of characters, words, lines, sentences, paragraphs, and pages contained in the document, and the average word length, average and maximum words per sentence, and the size of the document in bytes.

DOCUMENT INITIAL CODES

See INITIAL CODES

DOCUMENT SUMMARY

See SUMMARY, DOCUMENT

DOCUMENT WINDOW

See WINDOWS

DOS (ASCII) TEXT FILES

Retrieving a DOS Text File

Choose <u>F</u>ile, <u>O</u>pen (or SHIFT+F10)
Type the filename
Choose OK
Identify the file's format in the list box
Choose <u>S</u>elect

Retrieves a DOS (ASCII) text file to the screen. Useful once a file has been converted from another software program to a DOS text file, or if you wish to retrieve and then edit a DOS batch file already on disk. WordPerfect will attempt to identify the format of the file. In the File Format dialog box, the cursor will be located on the file format that WordPerfect has selected. If it is not correct, move the cursor to the correct format.

Saving as DOS Text File

Choose F̲ile, Save A̲s (or F10)
Type a filename
Fo̲rmat
Choose ASCII (Standard), ASCII (Stripped)
or DOS Delimited Text

Stores a file on disk as a DOS (ASCII) text file, stripping it
of any special formatting codes so the file can then be
used from DOS or transferred for use in another software
package. It is also useful when you wish to save a DOS
batch file to disk.

DOS, EXIT TO

Choose F̲ile, G̲o to Shell (or CTRL+F1)
G̲o to DOS or D̲OS Command

Exits temporarily to DOS so that you can type DOS
commands as desired. Select G̲o to DOS in order to
execute many commands; when you wish to return to
WordPerfect, type the word exit and press ENTER at the
DOS prompt.

Or, select D̲OS Command to execute a single DOS
command; afterwards, press any key to resume in
WordPerfect.

DOT LEADERS

See TABS, CENTER, and FLUSH RIGHT

DOWNLOADABLE (SOFT) FONTS

Defining Soft Fonts

Defines soft fonts that you have available for use with your printer as either Initially Present or Loaded During Print Job (see CARTRIDGES/FONTS/PRINT WHEELS for the command sequence).

Setting a Directory for Soft Fonts

Choose File, Print (or SHIFT+F7)
Select
Position cursor on a printer name
Edit, Directory for Soft Fonts
Type directory name

Indicates the drive and directory where WordPerfect should look to find downloadable font files.

Downloading Soft Fonts

Choose File, Print (or SHIFT+F7)
Initialize Printer, Continue

Clears any soft fonts from the printer's memory and loads soft fonts defined as Initially Present. Should be performed only once for each time the printer is turned on.

DRAG AND DROP

Block text
Click on block and drag to a new location
Release mouse button to move text or press CTRL and
    release mouse button to copy text

Moves or copies a block of text by "dragging" the text and "dropping" it into a new location. For methods to move or

copy text when not using a mouse, see COPY, COPY AND
PASTE, CUT, and CUT AND PASTE.

DRAW LINES

See LINE DRAW or GRAPHICS LINES

EDITING KEYS

See the "General Reminders" section

ENDNOTES

See FOOTNOTES/ENDNOTES

ENTER KEY

See RETURN

ENVELOPES

Lets you create envelopes from a letter onscreen as well
as on a blank screen. If a letter is onscreen, WordPerfect
will search for an address to use as the mailing address.
WordPerfect will use predefined envelope paper
definitions to create envelopes. If you do not see the
envelope type you need, you can easily create the
definition. WordPerfect can create POSTNET bar codes
on your envelopes based on 5-, 9- or 11-digit zip codes.

POSTNET bar codes speed the delivery of your presorted mail.

Changing Defaults in the Envelope Feature

Choose Layout, Envelope (or ALT+F12)
Setup (or SHIFT+F1)
Envelope Size
Select new default size and/or adjust
   Address Positions
Bar Code Creation
Select new default bar code option

Make the desired changes to the envelope defaults. The new settings will be saved and will remain in effect until changed again.

Creating an Envelope

Choose Layout, Envelope (or ALT+F12)
Envelope Size and select the desired envelope (omit step if current choice is OK)
Omit Return Address (omit step if current status is OK)
Return Address and type address (omit step if current return address is OK or if you want no address in order to print on a preprinted envelope)
Mailing Address and type address (omit step if WordPerfect selected an address that is OK)
Postnet Bar Code and indicate zip code for bar code pattern (omit step if current status is OK)
Choose Insert or Print

WordPerfect will create the envelope. It will be placed as a separate page at the end of the current document.

If you have more than one address in the active document, you can block the desired address first, then choose the envelope feature, to have WordPerfect select the correct address.

Creating a New Paper Definition for Envelopes

Choose Layout, Envelope (or ALT+F12)
Setup (or SHIFT+F1)
Envelope Size, Create
Create
Type name of new paper definition
Select Paper Type
Select Paper Size
Establish Paper Location
Enable/Disable Prompt to Load as desired
Select Orientation
Adjust Text for printer, if necessary

Make the desired selections in each of the option boxes.
The option to Adjust Text is used if your printer does not
honor the margins established by the paper definition.
Choosing this option makes it possible to adjust the text
on the print job while still making sure the image in view
mode corresponds to the printed output. (If you had
adjusted the margins, the representation of the envelope
in view mode would not be accurate.)

ENVIRONMENT

Choose File, Setup (or SHIFT+F1)
Environment

Alters settings that affect the working environment in
WordPerfect, including Backup Options, Beep Options,
Cursor Speed, Allow Undo, Format Document for Default
Printer on Open, Prompt for Hyphenation, Units of
Measure, Language, WordPerfect 5.1 Keyboard, Auto
Code Placement, WordPerfect 5.1 Cursor Movement, and
Delimited Text Options (see specific entries for details on
these options). Setup changes are saved to disk and
remain in effect until they are modified again.

EQUATIONS

Creates and edits a mathematical or scientific equation (see "Editing Boxes" in GRAPHICS BOXES). The Equations feature is a graphics editor. It does not solve equations.

Style Settings

Choose Graphics (or ALT+F9)
Graphics Boxes, Styles
List Styles from Document, Personal Library
  or Shared Library
Highlight Equation Box
Edit

Determines default options for the Equation Editor, including the equation's font size on the printed page; the equation's horizontal and vertical alignments; and a keyboard definition, if any, used to aid in creating the equation. These and other options can be altered for a specific equation by choosing Based on Box Style while in the Create/Edit Graphics Box dialog box.

ERROR MESSAGES

Self-explanatory prompts that indicate the wrong key was pressed or a command that you wish to execute cannot be performed. Common error messages and solutions include the following:

- "Backup File Exists": This message appears if, during your most recent WordPerfect working session, you experienced a power or machine failure or turned off the computer without exiting WordPerfect properly. In the error message dialog box, you will be given the option to Rename, Delete, or Open the backup file. See BACKUP.

- "Disk Full, Press Any Key to Continue": If you are attempting to save a file, delete some unwanted files on disk or insert another disk before you try again. If you are attempting to print, try printing from disk instead of from screen.

- "File Not Found": Try again to enter the proper filename or to indicate the proper drive or directory where the file is stored.

- "Insufficient File Handles to Run WordPerfect": Include the FILES=20 (or higher) command that must be present in the CONFIG.SYS file to run WordPerfect. Then restart your computer.

- "Not Enough Memory": If your document is large, split it into smaller files; consider using the Master Document feature. If you are working with more than one document, close any files you don't need at the moment. If you started WordPerfect from Shell, consider restarting WordPerfect from DOS. You may want to purchase more memory for your computer. WordPerfect 6.0 works with both expanded and extended memory.

- "WP Disk Full, Press Any Key to Continue": Redirect overflow files to a disk containing more free space using the /D startup option (see STARTUP (SLASH) OPTIONS). Consider purchasing a larger hard disk for your computer.

ESCAPE KEY

See REPEAT

EXIT DOCUMENT

Choose File, Exit (or F7)
Yes to save document (in which case you must indicate or confirm a filename) or No to exit without saving the document.

Yes to exit the document and document window, or No to exit the document but remain in the document window.

Clears the document currently onscreen and exits the document window. (When only one document window is open, this command lets you exit WordPerfect.)

You can also exit a document and document window using the Close command. (See CLOSE DOCUMENT.)

EXIT WORDPERFECT

See "Starting and Ending a WordPerfect Session" in the "General Reminders" section.

FAST SAVE

Choose File, Save As (or F10)
Setup (or SHIFT+F1)
Fast Save (to disable or enable)

Indicates to WordPerfect whether or not to save files without formatting for the printer before doing so. This speeds up the time it takes to save a document. However, it will take longer to print an unformatted document from disk, because the document must be formatted first.

By default, this option is enabled during the installation process. Changes made to the Fast Save option remain in effect until you modify the option again.

FAXING DOCUMENTS

Lets you send WordPerfect documents as faxes via the fax/modem installed in your computer. It is available only if you have both the hardware and the supporting communications software. If the software is not present, the feature will not be enabled on the print menu. Also, if your fax/modem is controlled by a terminate-and-stay-resident (TSR) program, WordPerfect's Fax Services feature will not work.

Options included in the Fax Services feature include faxing the active document, faxing a document on disk, binary file transfer (your fax/modem and the recipient's fax device must have this capability in order to use this feature), a phone book to record the numbers that you fax to most frequently, sending faxes to groups, a utility to view the status of a fax currently in progress, a send log, and a retrieve log. You can also set a specified date and time to send a fax on disk.

Canceling a Fax

Choose File, Print (or SHIFT+F7)
Fax Services, Fax Activity
Cancel Current Fax

Faxing the Document

Choose File, Print (or SHIFT+F7)
Fax Services
Mark Phonebook Entry with an asterisk or choose
   Manual Dial, type the required information, choose OK
Choose options from Send Fax dialog box
Choose Send Fax

The file will be renamed and saved on disk with the extension .FAX.

You can also send a fax from a document on disk by typing the name of the file (or choose it from the File List or Quicklist) and choose Send File. In order to send a file from disk, the file must first have been saved in the fax format (rasterized). Use the option "Save as an image for Fax on Disk". The file will be saved with .FAX as the extension.

Using the Phone Book

Choose File, Print (or SHIFT+F7)
Fax Services, Phonebook

You can create an entry or create a group. The
individuals included in a group must also exist as
separate entries in the phone book. You can also select
another phone book.

FILE LIST

Choose File, File Manager (or F5)
or
Choose File List in a dialog box that lists this option.

Lets you list a single file, file pattern, or specific
directory for use in the File Manager or in another dialog
box where this feature appears. See also FILE
MANAGER.

FILE MANAGER

Choose File, File Manager (or F5)
Type the name of the desired directory (or use Quicklist,
    Quickfinder or Directory Tree) to indicate the name
Choose OK

The File Manager can be used to browse through lists of
files; search for files based on specified criteria; view the
contents of a file; open/retrieve files; print files; change
the default directory for the current WordPerfect session;
create and delete directories; perform file management
tasks such as copying, moving, renaming and deleting
files; and determine the remaining storage space
available on a specified disk.

Many of the features of the File Manager are covered in detail in other sections of this book. See also COPY, DELETE FILES, DIRECTORY, FIND FILES, LOOK, MOVE/RENAME FILES, OPEN DOCUMENT, PRINT, RETRIEVE DOCUMENT, and SUMMARY, DOCUMENT.

Customizing the File Manager Setup

Choose File, File Manager (or F5)
Type the name of the desired directory
Choose OK
Setup (or SHIFT+F1)

Lets you choose desired options for how File Manager should appear, what files should appear, and how files should be sorted.

Navigating in the File Manager

Use the "Parent Directory" listing at the top of each file list to move back (up) one level in the directory structure. To move forward (down) one level to a subdirectory of the current directory, select the subdirectory name.

Use the arrow keys to move the cursor to a particular file or directory name. You can also use HOME, HOME, UP ARROW to move to the beginning of the list, and HOME, HOME, DOWN ARROW to move to the end of the list. Or, use the mouse to scroll through the list.

Use Name Search to move the cursor to a particular file name. Type **N**, then begin typing the filename. Notice that the first character you type will move your cursor to the first filename that begins with that letter. It may not be necessary to type the entire filename in order to move your cursor to the correct filename. Then press ENTER to end Name Search.

Using a File Pattern to List Files

Use the "Current Directory" listing and the DOS wildcard symbols to narrow down the list of files to a file pattern. For example, if you were looking at a list of files contained in the C:\WPDOCS directory and wished to see only a list of files beginning with the letter *F*, in File Manager:

Highlight "Current Directory"
Press ENTER
Modify directory name to C:\WPDOCS\F*.*
Press ENTER

The file listing would then be modified so that the list contained only the files whose names began with the letter *F*. See also FIND FILES. In a file pattern, ? represents one character and * represents any number of characters.

FILENAME ON STATUS LINE

See DISPLAY

FILL STYLES

Lets you indicate a background shading for graphics elements, including graphics boxes and borders. Shaded, colored, and gradient fills are available—subject, of course, to your printer's ability to support those features. A gradient fill combines two colors in a predefined pattern, Linear, Radial, or Rectangular.

Choosing Predefined Fill Styles

Choose Graphics (or ALT+F9)
Choose a graphics element (such as Borders, Paragraph)
Fill Style
Highlight desired fill style
Select

Specifies the fill style for a particular graphics element.

Modifying Fill Styles

Choose Graphics (or ALT+F9)
Fill Styles

Lets you create or edit a fill style for all graphics
elements that use that style. You can modify the color
and fill pattern. You can also modify a fill style when
displaying the Fill Styles dialog box for a particular
graphics element.

FIND FILES

Choose File, File Manager (or F5)
Type drive or directory name
Choose OK
Find
Name, Document Summary, First Page, Entire Document,
   Conditions, Quickfinder or Undo

Rewrites the File Manager screen, displaying only those
files that meet certain conditions. The conditions you can
specify include the following:

- A certain word pattern (one or more words) in a document summary

- A certain word pattern in the document's first page of
  text

- A certain word pattern anywhere within the document

- A certain date when the file was last saved on disk

- Any combination of the above conditions

- A certain character pattern in the file's name, such as
  "LT", which would find the files LT059, JONES.LTR, and
  ALTMAN.

Use this to find a file or group of files on a specific drive
or in a specific directory.

The word pattern can contain one or more words. For two words separated by a comma, WordPerfect searches for documents that contain either word. For two words separated by a space or semicolon (;), WordPerfect searches for documents that contain both words. For words within quotation marks, WordPerfect searches for documents that contain that exact phrase.

For the Document Summary, First Page, or Entire Document menu item, type in the word pattern you wish to search on. For the Conditions menu item, a File Manager Find Conditions dialog box appears so you can specify more than one search condition; after specifying the conditions, select the OK button to begin the search, or select the Reset menu item to undo the current search conditions.

You can limit the search to selected files by marking them with an asterisk before selecting Find (see MARK FILES).

FLOATING CELL

See TABLES

FLUSH RIGHT

Choose Layout, Alignment, Flush Right (or ALT+F6)

Places a short line of text flush against the right margin and is useful to align dates or memorandum headings.

To make text flush right as you type, choose Flush Right (ALT+F6), type the text, and then press ENTER to move down to a new line.

To flush right existing text, position the cursor on the first character, choose Flush Right (ALT+F6), and then press the DOWN ARROW key. If you first use the Block feature to highlight a section of text and then choose

Flush Right, numerous lines can be aligned flush right all at once (see also JUSTIFICATION).

Choose Flush Right twice in a row to precede the text with dot leaders (....).

FONT

Allows you to change the appearance, size, or typeface for the characters in your document.

Setting Attributes for a Font

On the printed page, alters the appearance or size of the text for the current font. For instance, boldface, underline, and large are all font attributes (see APPEARANCE and SIZE ATTRIBUTE RATIOS).

The fonts available for selection depend on your printer's built-in fonts and on the fonts you mark as available on printer cartridges or soft fonts (see CARTRIDGES/FONTS/PRINT WHEELS). In addition to these printer fonts, graphics fonts are available, some of which are packaged with WordPerfect. Graphics fonts are also used as screen fonts when you are working in graphics mode or text mode, so that you can see a representation of how the font will appear on the printed page.

Setting Attributes Back to Normal

Choose Font, Normal (CTRL+N)

After turning on appearance or size attributes, turns off all appearance and size attributes at one time so that text returns to normal for the current font. You can block text and then turn off attributes for only that section of text.

Setting the Current Font

Choose F<u>o</u>nt, F<u>o</u>nt (or CTRL+F8)
<u>F</u>ont
Select the font of your choice

Alters the font for regular text in a particular section of a document. When a document is first created, the current font is set as whatever has been established as the initial font for that document.

Position the cursor anywhere within the document to alter the current font starting at that location. Or, block text before changing the current font for a section of text.

Setting Downloadable Fonts

See DOWNLOADABLE (SOFT) FONTS

Setting the Initial Font

Choose <u>L</u>ayout (or SHIFT+F8)
<u>D</u>ocument, Initial <u>F</u>ont
<u>F</u>ont
Select the font of your choice
Press ENTER
<u>S</u>ize
Select the desired font size
Press ENTER
<u>C</u>urrent Document Only or <u>A</u>ll New Documents

Alters the font for all text—including regular text, headers, footers, footnotes, endnotes, and captions—for either the current document or for all new documents. If you choose <u>A</u>ll New Documents, the font you specify will be assumed for all new documents that you create (using the current printer).

FOOTERS

See HEADERS/FOOTERS

FOOTNOTES/ENDNOTES

Creating Footnotes/Endnotes

Choose Layout, Footnote or Endnote (or CTRL+F7)
Create
Press F7 when finished typing text

Inserts a note reference number in the main text, which
will appear as a superscript when printed. The text of a
footnote appears at the bottom of the same page as the
note reference number. The text of an endnote appears at
the end of the document, unless you use the Endnote
Placement feature (see "Endnote Placement").

You can also paste text and retrieve files into footnotes
and endnotes.

Editing Footnotes/Endnotes

Choose Layout, Footnote or Endnote (or CTRL+F7)
Edit
Type number of footnote/endnote to be edited

Edits a previously created footnote or endnote. The note
text appears on the screen for editing. If you want to edit
other footnotes or endnotes during the same session, you
can use HOME, PAGE UP or HOME, PAGE DOWN to access
the previous or next note.

Endnote Placement

Choose Layout, Endnote(or CTRL+F7)
Placement
Yes to restart numbering below the endnotes at 1, or No to
    continue consecutive numbering

Specifies a location where all endnotes that have been
created prior to that location should be printed. Endnotes
created beyond that location will print at the end of the
document (or at the next endnote placement location).

WordPerfect marks the endnote placement location in the document window by displaying the following comment in a single-line box: "Endnote Placement".

Renumbering Footnotes/Endnotes

Choose Layout, Endnote(or CTRL+F7)
New Number
Type new beginning number

Renumbers all footnotes or endnotes beyond the cursor position. After typing the new beginning number in the Set Footnote Number dialog box, the other options that can be set include: Numbering Method (Numbers, Lower Letters, Upper Letters, Lower Roman, Upper Roman, Characters), Increment Number, Decrement Number, Display in Document.

Setting Options

Choose Layout, Endnote(or CTRL+F7)
Options

Alters any of the initial settings for how footnotes or endnotes will appear in a particular printed document, including the following:

- Spacing Between Footnotes/Endnotes: The spacing (such as single or double spacing) within and between footnotes or endnotes.

- Amount of Footnote/Endnotes to Keep Together: The amount of a footnote or endnote to keep together on one page if the note in its entirety cannot fit on one page, so that the second half must continue on the following page.

Also allows for changing additional initial settings for footnotes only, including the following:

- Footnote Separator Line: Allows you to change the line separating text from the footnotes.

- Restart Footnote Numbers Each Page: Reset footnote numbers to 1 on every page.

- Footnote at <u>B</u>ottom of Page: Determines whether footnotes will print at the bottom of the page or immediately following the reference text (in the event that the text does not occupy a full page).

- Print <u>C</u>ontinued Message: Whether or not a "(Continued)" message prints at the end of the page and the beginning of the next page if a footnote must be split between two pages.

FORCE ODD/EVEN PAGE

Choose <u>L</u>ayout (or SHIFT+F8)
<u>P</u>age
<u>F</u>orce Page
<u>O</u>dd, <u>E</u>ven, Ne<u>w</u> or <u>N</u>one

Forces the page number on the current page to be odd, even, or on a new page. The New option can be used instead of a hard page break. This avoids the potential problem of having a blank page print if a soft page break should occur before the hard page break.

FOREIGN LANGUAGES

See LANGUAGE

FORMAT

Choose <u>L</u>ayout (or SHIFT+F8)

Provides access to the options that alter format settings. A format code affects a document beginning at the location of the code and continuing either to the next code of the same type or to the end of the document.

Position the cursor on the Document Initial Codes screen or at the top of the document to alter the format starting at the beginning of the document. You also can position the cursor anywhere within the document to alter the format starting at that location.

You can format characters, lines, pages, documents, and numerous other items through the Layout menu. You will find details under the specific item you wish to format or the option name on the Layout menu.

FORMS

See PAPER DEFINITIONS

FRAME

See WINDOWS

FUNCTION KEYS

Provides access to WordPerfect features and commands. See the "General Reminders" section for a list of the key names corresponding to each of the function keys. To display a list of function key names in the form of a template, use the Template option from the Help menu (see HELP).

GENERATE CROSS-REFERENCES, INDEXES, LISTS, AND TABLES

Choose Tools (or ALT+F5)
Generate
Enable or disable Save Modified Subdocuments
Choose OK

Updates cross-references if you edit your text after you mark references and targets (see CROSS-REFERENCE). Also creates (or replaces) lists, tables, or an index once you have marked the text and defined the format for the lists, tables, or index (see LISTS, TABLES OF AUTHORITIES, TABLES OF CONTENTS, and INDEXES). Lets you specify whether you wish to save modified subdocuments that may be part of the document (see MASTER DOCUMENTS).

GO TO

Swiftly moves the cursor to specific locations in a document or in text columns (see the "General Reminders" section).

GO TO DOS

See DOS, EXIT TO

GO TO SHELL

See SHELL, EXIT TO

GRAMMAR CHECKER

WordPerfect 6.0 ships with a grammar checking program called Grammatik 5. You can check a document that is already in the active document window, or you can start the grammar checker, then identify the file to be checked. The opening screen provides you with a pull-down menu system from which you can set preferences for the grammar check. You can also choose an Interactive check or Statistics check from the opening screen without opening the pull-down menus.

Through the Preferences menu, it is possible to modify the style rules used for the grammar check, based upon the type of document you are writing. For example, to check a business memo, a report for a scientific journal, and a letter to your mother, you would probably want to use three different style rules.

An extensive help system is built into the Grammatik program. You can choose help by pressing F1.

Performing an Interactive Check

Choose <u>T</u>ools, <u>W</u>riting Tools (or ALT+F1)
<u>G</u>rammatik
<u>I</u>nteractive

Grammatik will pause when it detects an error and wait for you to correct or bypass the error. The following table explains the options for the interactive check:

Key	Description
F1	Go to the Help feature
F5	Ignore the rule class for the phrase only
F6	Ignore the rule class for the document
F9	Edit the error or recheck the corrected text from the cursor position
F10	Proceed to the next problem
ESC	Exit from the grammar checking session

Performing a Statistics Check

Retrieve document into the active document window
Choose Tools, Writing Tools (or ALT+F1)
Grammatik
Statistics

You will receive statistics concerning the readability of
your document based on two indicators, Flesch-Kincaid
and Gunning's Fog Index. Many writers become
unnerved by the grade-level indicator. Remember that
this indicates the grade level required of the *reader* to
understand your document. For most business memos,
seventh or eighth grade level is a good goal. This grade
level indicates that your document is concise, to the
point, and easy to understand.

GRAPHICS BOXES

Allows you to incorporate a box that contains either text,
an equation, an image, or nothing into a document. There
are eight predefined graphics box styles to choose from:
Figure, Text, Table, User, Equation, Button, Watermark
Image, and In-Line Equation. Each style has a different
set of default characteristics.

Creating Boxes

Choose Graphics (or ALT+F9)
Graphics Boxes, Create
Based on Box Style
Select graphics box style
Contents
Image, Image on Disk, Text, Equation, or None

You can retrieve into the box using the Filename option.
Or, you can type text directly into the box with the
Create Text option. To create a caption for the box,
choose the Create Caption option, change the default

caption if you wish, and press F7 to exit. Options allows you to change the caption style.

Other items are predefined but can be changed. You can edit the border/fill in the box; attach the box to a character, paragraph, or page; edit the box position; edit the box size; and edit the text flow around the box.

When working in text mode, after a graphics box is created, a box outline, but not the box contents, appears in the document window. The box contents are visible in graphics and page modes, in Print Preview, and on the printed page.

Editing Boxes

Choose Graphics (or ALT+F9)
Graphics Boxes, Edit
Select the box to be edited
Choose Edit Box

Edits the definition of a previously created graphics box. In the Edit Graphics Box dialog box, you can redefine the box characteristics, such as the position or size.

You can also edit the box contents. Choose Image Editor, Edit Text, Create Text, or Edit Equation to edit the box contents. How the Editor operates depends on the box contents.

- If the box contents indicate "text", use the Editor to type or edit the text.

- If the box contents indicate "graphics image", use the Editor to move, scale, rotate, or invert the image displayed onscreen.

- If the box contents indicate "equation", use the Editor to create and format mathematical and scientific equations. The Equation Editor is composed of three windows: the editing window, where you type and edit the text of the equation; the equation palette, from which you can select commands and special symbols for insertion into the equation; and the display window, where the final result can be viewed. Use the F5 key to choose items from the equation palette; press F5 twice to change the equation palette.

If you use a mouse, you can change a box's position or size without using the command sequence above. Simply click the box, then drag the box to move it, or drag a sizing handle to size the box.

Modifying Box Styles

Choose Graphics (or ALT+F9)
Graphics Boxes, Styles

Alters any of the initial settings for the style of a particular box, such as a Figure box or Table box. This affects all graphics boxes using that style in your document. While creating or editing a graphics box, you can also modify a box style if you choose Based on Box Style and then choose to edit a particular style. Defaults include content and caption options, the border/fill for the box, how the box is attached to the document, the position and size of the box, and how text flows around the box.

Renumbering Boxes

Choose Graphics (or ALT+F9)
Graphics Boxes, Numbering
Highlight the appropriate box style
Set Method
Numbers, Lower Letter, Upper Letter,
    Lower Roman, Upper Roman
Set Value (only if you wish to start
    at a different value than what
    WordPerfect has chosen)

Renumbers the captions of all graphics boxes of a particular style beyond the cursor position. Note that this does not affect the numbering of the boxes themselves on the editing screen when you are working in text mode. The boxes will continue to be identified in sequential order as Box 1, Box 2, and so on. To see the effect of the new caption numbering scheme, use graphics or page mode, Print Preview, or print the document.

GRAPHICS LINES

Choose Graphics (or ALT+F9)
Graphics Boxes, Graphics Line
Create

Inserts a horizontal or vertical line at the cursor. WordPerfect displays a dialog box in which you define the line's characteristics. The graphics line displays on the printed page but not in the document window if you are working in text mode. You can determine the line orientation (horizontal or vertical), position, thickness, length, line style, color, and spacing. If you choose Line Style, you can create or edit a line style for all graphics elements that use that style.

GRAPHICS QUALITY

See TEXT/GRAPHICS QUALITY

HANGING INDENT

See INDENT

HARD PAGE

See PAGE BREAKS

HARD RETURN

See RETURN

HARD SPACE

HOME, SPACEBAR

Inserts a space that "glues" two words together so they will not be split up by word wrap. Useful for keeping the text of an address or date on the same line.

HEADERS/FOOTERS

Creating Headers/Footers

Choose Layout (or SHIFT+F8)
Header/Footer/Watermark
Headers or Footers
A or B
All Pages, Even Pages, or Odd Pages
Create
Type text for header/footer
Press F7

Inserts standard lines of text at the top of pages (header) or at the bottom of pages (footer). Use page mode, Print Preview, or print the document to see the effect of the header or footer. Headers and footers are not displayed in the document window in text mode.

Make sure to position the cursor on the first page where you want the header or footer to print before following the command sequence. It is possible to establish page numbering in a header (see PAGE NUMBERING for the procedure). See SUPPRESS FOR CURRENT PAGE for the procedure to suppress headers and footers for a specific page in a document.

Discontinuing Headers/Footers

Choose Layout (or SHIFT+F8)
Header/Footer/Watermark
Header or Footer
A or B
All Pages, Even Pages, or Odd Pages
Off

Discontinues the header or footer specified to the end of the document (or until the next header or footer of that type is created farther ahead in the text).

Editing Headers/Footers

Choose Layout (or SHIFT+F8)
Header/Footer/Watermark
Header or Footer
A or B
All Pages, Even Pages, or Odd Pages
Edit

Edits a header or footer that you previously created and whose code is located above the cursor position.

HELP

Choose Help (or F1)
Contents, Index, How do I, Coaches, Macros
    Tutorial, or WP Info

Provides online assistance with the functions and features of WordPerfect. Help is also context-sensitive, so if you press F1 while in a dialog box, a help screen describing the options for that dialog box will be displayed. The Help options are as follows:

- Contents: A list of all of the help features available on the initial Help menu as well as a glossary of terms, a keyboard template, a list of keystrokes for moving the cursor, a list of shortcut key commands, and a list of error messages, their causes, and possible solutions.

- Index: A list of help topics. Highlight the desired topic and press ENTER to view the help documentation.

- How do I: A list of the most commonly performed tasks. Highlight the desired topic and press ENTER to get step-by-step instructions for performing common tasks in WordPerfect.

- Coaches: An interactive tutorial that guides you through the performance of tasks in the current document.

- Macros: A list of topics pertaining only to macros, from simple tasks to complex programming commands. Highlight the desired topic and press ENTER to view the Macro help documentation.

- Tutorial: A set of lessons covering the basic skills needed to create documents in WordPerfect. The tutorial offers you a choice of learning mouse or keyboard techniques. Follow the instructions on the screen to go to the next screen or to exit.

- WP Info: A display of your registration number (if it was entered during the installation process), information about the version and release date of your WordPerfect installation, where critical WordPerfect program files are located, and the current status of system resources, such as memory usage.

HIDDEN TEXT

Marks text to be hidden. Useful when you wish to include questions, messages, comments, or answers to tests within the document. When hidden text is shown, it is treated like other text; it can be edited or printed. When it is hidden, text collapses into a code.

For Existing Text

Block the text
Choose Font, Hidden Text, Hidden Text

The Hidden Text attribute will be applied only to the text in the block.

For Text About to Be Typed

Choose Font, Hidden Text, Hidden Text to turn it on
Type the text
Choose Font, Hidden Text, Hidden Text to turn it off

When you turn off the Hidden Text feature, the cursor is moved to the right of the "Hidden Text Off" code. In addition to using the menu commands, as described above, you can also tap the RIGHT ARROW key.

Hiding/Showing Text

Font, Hidden Text, Show All Hidden Text

Place an X in the checkbox to show all hidden text in the document. Remove the X to keep the text hidden.

HIGHLIGHT TEXT

See BLOCK

HORIZONTAL SCROLL BAR

See SCROLL BARS

HYPERTEXT

Creating a Link

Block the text or symbols in your document that
   will represent the hypertext jump location
Choose Tools, Hypertext
Create Link
Go to Bookmark (you will have to identify the
   name of the bookmark to which you are
   linking) or Go to Other Document (you will
   have to identify the name, including path,
   of the other document, as well as the name
   of the bookmark to which you are linking)
   or Run Macro
Hypertext Appearance
Highlighted Text or Button

Link sections of your document to other sections in the
same document, other documents, or to macros, to run
them automatically from within a document. Before
hypertext links can be established, create bookmarks in
the document and the macros that will be executed from
the document. (See BOOKMARK.)

Jumping to Hypertext

Move the cursor to the hypertext location
Choose Tools, Hypertext
Jump/Run

(If you want WordPerfect to move the cursor to the
hypertext location, choose Tools, Hypertext, Go to Next
Link.)

Returning from the Jump

Choose Tools, Hypertext
Return from Jump

HYPHEN TYPES

Character

HYPHEN

Inserts a hyphen that will remain between two words. The words may be split on separate lines by word wrap if they fall at the end of a line.

Dash Character (Hard Hyphen)

HOME, HYPHEN

Inserts a hyphen that "glues" two words together so they will not be split up by word wrap. Useful to serve as a minus sign in an equation or for keeping hyphenated phrases (such as mother-in-law) on the same line (see also HARD SPACE).

Soft Hyphen

CTRL+SHIFT+HYPHEN

Inserts a hyphen that will appear only if a word falls at the end of a line in the Hyphenation Zone so that it requires hyphenation. This is useful if you wish to perform manual hyphenation. The hyphen disappears if you edit the text and the word no longer falls at the end of a line (see also HYPHENATION).

HYPHENATION

Turning On/Off

Choose Layout (or SHIFT+F8)
Line, Hyphenation

Turns hyphenation on or off. You can turn on hyphenation before you type a document or after typing.

Position the cursor at the top of the document (or where you want hyphenation to begin) before following the command sequence.

When hyphenation is off, words that do not fit within the Hyphenation Zone are wrapped down to the next line. When hyphenation is on, WordPerfect checks for hyphenation candidates that fall within the Hyphenation Zone as you type or move the cursor through existing text. WordPerfect hyphenates a word by inserting a soft hyphen.

Depending on how you set up hyphenation to operate (see ENVIRONMENT), WordPerfect may prompt you for the hyphen location.

HYPHENATION ZONE

Choose Layout (or SHIFT+F8)
Line, Hyphenation Zone

Determines the position boundaries within which word hyphenation will occur when hyphenation is on. The left and right Hyphenation Zone boundaries are expressed as a percentage of the line length from the right margin location. A word will be hyphenated if it starts at or before the left Hyphenation Zone and extends past the right Hyphenation Zone.

Enter left and right Hyphenation Zone settings as a percent of the line length. If you reduce the left or right Hyphenation Zone percent settings, this narrows the Hyphenation Zone so that more words will become hyphenation candidates. If you increase a percent setting, fewer words become hyphenation candidates.

IBM CHARACTER SET

Use the IBM Character Set to place characters in your document that are not available from the normal keyboard. Hold the ALT key down and type the ASCII number for the character on the number pad; release the ALT key and the character will appear on your screen. (Some characters will appear as small, reverse-video triangles if you are working in text mode.) For example, to place a medium-sized bullet (•) in your document, hold the ALT key and type 7 on the numeric key pad; release the ALT key.

INDENT

Back Tab Indent

Choose Layout, Alignment, Back Tab (or SHIFT+TAB)

Indents the first line in a paragraph one tab stop to the left, which is backwards from the usual. If the cursor is at the left margin when SHIFT+TAB is pressed, the cursor moves to the tab stop left of the left margin.

Hanging Indent

Choose Layout, Alignment, Hanging Indent

Indents all but the first line of text in a paragraph one tab stop to the right. Leaves the first line "hanging." You can also press F4 and then SHIFT+TAB to create a hanging indent.

Left Indent

Choose Layout, Alignment, Indent-> (F4)

Indents the left side of a paragraph (text that ends with a hard return code). The paragraph is indented one tab stop to the right each time you press F4. This is useful for

indenting a whole paragraph of text following a
paragraph number or bullet.

Left/Right Indent

Choose Layout, Alignment, Indent ->< (SHIFT+F4)

Indents both sides of a paragraph. The left side of the
paragraph is indented one tab stop each time you press
SHIFT+F4, and the right side is indented by an equal
amount. Useful for indenting a long quote.

INDEXES

Creating a Concordance File

Type the word or phrase to be included in an index and press
ENTER, so there is only one entry on each line.
Save the concordance file as you would a regular document.

Avoids the need to mark a phrase individually every time
it occurs in a document. When the index is generated,
WordPerfect will search the document for all phrases
contained in the concordance file—just as if you marked
each one yourself—and include the corresponding page
numbers in the index. Creating a concordance file does
not exclude your marking words or phrases individually
in the text.

When WordPerfect generates the index, the concordance
file phrases are assumed to be headings. To denote
certain phrases as subheadings, mark those phrases in
the concordance file just as you mark text in the
document. (See "Mark Text.")

Defining the Index

Choose Tools, Index (or ALT+F5)
Define

Defines the location and page numbering style of the index. The index will be generated in the location where your cursor is positioned.

Generating the Index

Generates an index after you have marked the entries for the index (and/or created a concordance file) and defined the index (see GENERATE CROSS-REFERENCES, INDEXES, LISTS, AND TABLES for the command sequence).

Marking Text

Block the text to be included in the index
Choose Tools, Index (or ALT+F5)
To mark as a heading, choose OK, or to include as a
    subheading, choose Subheading.

Marks a word or phrase you wish to be included in the index when generated. When the blocked text is placed in the heading and subheading fields in the Mark Text dialog box, that is a suggestion only. The blocked text and heading/subheading do not have to match. You can type in the appropriate headings and subheadings that correspond with the blocked text.

INITIAL CODES

Setting for Document Onscreen

Choose Layout (or SHIFT+F8)
Document
Document Initial Codes
Insert desired formatting codes
Press F7

Controls the default format settings for the document currently onscreen. Codes on the Document Initial Codes screen override the initial codes setup. Conversely, codes on the Document Initial Codes screen can be overridden by any format codes placed later in the text of the document.

It is useful to insert format codes on the Document Initial Codes screen, rather than in the document itself, when you wish to activate a format change starting at the beginning of a document; it reduces the potential clutter of codes at the top of a document. Codes on this screen affect not only the main body of a document, but elements such as footnotes, endnotes, headers, and footers.

Setting for New Documents

Choose Layout (or SHIFT+F8)
Document
Initial Codes Setup
Insert desired formatting codes
Press F7

Controls the default format settings for every new document created. Format codes that you insert on the Initial Codes Setup screen override the initial format settings as set up by WordPerfect. The initial format settings as set up by WordPerfect include, for instance, 1-inch margins, single spacing, and tabs every 1/2 inch.

However, codes inserted on the Setup Initial Codes screen can be overridden by any format codes placed on the Document Initial Codes screen, or directly in the actual text of the document.

It is useful to insert format codes on the Setup Initial Codes screen when you wish to activate a format change for the majority of documents that you will create from now on.

INITIAL FONT

See FONT

INITIAL SETTINGS

Except for those features whose initial settings are controlled through the Setup menu, initial settings for features are handled at the feature level. For example, if you wanted to modify the initial settings for all print jobs, you would choose File, Print/Fax, Setup; you would then make the desired initial setting changes within the Print/Fax dialog box. (See also COLOR ON SCREEN, DISPLAY, ENVIRONMENT, KEYBOARD LAYOUT, LOCATION OF FILES, and MOUSE, all of which are options on the Setup menu.)

Initial settings for the layout of a document are controlled using the Initial Codes feature. (See INITIAL CODES.) Initial settings for the font used in a document are controlled using the Initial Font feature. (See FONT.)

INITIALIZE PRINTER

See DOWNLOADABLE (SOFT) FONTS

INSERT MODE

INS (only necessary if currently in Typeover mode)

Characters you type are inserted at the cursor, and existing characters are pushed to the right to make room for the new characters. The INS key is a toggle that switches between Insert and Typeover modes. (See also TYPEOVER MODE.)

INTERNATIONAL CHARACTERS

See COMPOSE or SPECIAL CHARACTERS

ITALICS

Prints text in italics (cursive and slanted to the right), based on the current font. In text mode, the italics will be displayed on the screen in a different color or brightness to distinguish it from normal text. (See also COLORS ON SCREEN to set the way that the italics attribute is displayed onscreen.) In graphics or page layout modes, the characters will actually appear in italics.

For Existing Text

Block the text
Choose Font, Italics (or CTRL+I)

The Italics attribute will be applied only to the text in the block.

For Text About to Be Typed

Font, Italics (or CTRL+I) to turn on italics
Type the text
Font, Italics (or CTRL+I) to turn off italics

When you turn off the Italics feature, the cursor is moved to the right of the "Italics Off" code. In addition to using the menu commands or pressing CTRL+I as described above, you can also tap the RIGHT ARROW key.

JUSTIFICATION

Choose Layout, Justification
Left, Center, Right, Full, or Full, All Lines

Determines how text is aligned in relation to the left and right margins. Left justification results in an even left margin and a ragged right margin; right justification has the opposite effect. Center justification positions each line equidistant from the left and right margins. Full justification results in extra spaces being inserted on each line in paragraphs to make both the left and right margin even when the text is printed. Full, All Lines allows you to evenly space all letters of a title or heading between the margins.

You can see the effect of full justification by choosing graphics or page mode, or by printing or previewing the document.

KEEP TEXT TOGETHER

See BLOCK PROTECT, CONDITIONAL END OF PAGE, WIDOW/ORPHAN PROTECTION, and HARD SPACE

KERNING

Choose Layout (or SHIFT+F8)
Other, Printer Functions
Kerning

Allows for the reduction of space between certain letter pairs, such as WA or VO. The kerning is based on the kerning tables for the printer that is used to print out your document. (Not all printers have defined kerning tables, so kerning may have no effect on your document.)

KEYBOARD LAYOUT

Creating a Keyboard Layout

Choose File, Setup (or SHIFT+F1)
Keyboard Layout
Create

Establishes a keyboard definition, where a keyboard
definition alters the function assigned by WordPerfect
Corporation to one or more keys on the keyboard. Within
a keyboard definition, keys such as [, ALT+1, CTRL+S, or
SHIFT+F2 can be defined to activate a certain command,
insert a special character, or execute a macro. Once you
create a keyboard definition, it will only become active
when you select it (see "Select"). This is useful for
tailoring the keyboard to your personal needs.

When the Keyboard Name dialog box appears, enter a
filename for the keyboard definition you are about to
create; WordPerfect automatically assigns the extension
.WPK to that filename. Next, select Create to create an
assignment for a certain key. In the Create Key dialog
box, type the character or key combination to which the
new character/task/feature should be assigned. Select
Description to create or edit an explanation of that key's
assignment. Assign an action type, Text, Command, or
Macro. If you choose Macro, you will also have to either
Create/Edit Macro, Retrieve Macro, or Save Macro.

It is also possible to create/edit a keyboard with the Map
feature.

Drive/Directory Location

Determines where, on disk, the keyboard definition files
(with the file extension .WPK) are stored. (See
LOCATION OF FILES.)

Managing a Keyboard Layout

Choose File, Setup (or SHIFT+F1)
Keyboard Layout
Select, Create, Edit, Delete, Copy, Rename,
    Map, Name Search

Allows you to manipulate existing key definitions. You
can delete, rename, or copy a definition by positioning
the cursor on a keyboard definition name and selecting
the corresponding menu item. Or, edit a keyboard
definition by positioning the cursor and selecting Edit.
You can view a map of all the keys that have been
reassigned (except for function and cursor movement
keys) by positioning the cursor and selecting Map. The
Map menu item also allows you to alter key assignments.
If you select the Name Search menu item, you can
position the cursor on a keyboard definition without
using the arrow keys; instead, type the beginning letters
of the key definition name until the cursor moves there.
Press ENTER to end Name Search.

Selecting a Keyboard Layout

Choose File, Setup (or SHIFT+F1)
Keyboard Layout
Position cursor on keyboard definition name
Select

Turns on (selects) a specific keyboard definition. Once a
keyboard definition is selected, all keys abide by their
assigned function. In addition to the "normal" keyboard,
to which functions have been assigned by WordPerfect
Corporation, three other programmed keyboards are
available: CUA, Equation, and Macro. These keyboards
have special functions assigned to various ALT+Letter
and CTRL+Letter combinations to make certain tasks
easier. For example, the Macro keyboard has the bullet
macro assigned to the ALT+B key combination.

LABELS

Choose Layout (or SHIFT+F8)
Page, Labels
Highlight Predefined Label, Choose Select (only necessary
    the first time you use the feature)
Highlight name of the required label
Select
Make any needed changes in the Labels Printer
    Info dialog box

Properly formats a document containing addresses for
printing on mailing labels. Each label is separated from
the next label by a hard page break (CTRL+ENTER).

LANGUAGE

Choose Layout (SHIFT+F8)
Other, Language

Indicates to WordPerfect you wish to use the formatting
conventions of the selected language for the date, sort,
footnote, and tables features. Indicate the two-letter
code for the language you desire from the list that
appears. To use the language feature with the dictionary,
thesaurus, hyphenation, and Grammatik, you will have to
purchase another language module.

LEADING

Choose Layout (SHIFT+F8)
Other, Printer Functions
Leading Adjustment

Dictates the amount of extra space between lines of text,
which is in addition to the 2 points of leading

automatically added for proportionally spaced fonts. (Leading for monospaced fonts is built in.)

Enter a leading measurement both for lines that end with soft return codes (those within paragraphs) and for lines that end with hard return codes (those that separate paragraphs).

LINE DRAW

Choose Graphics, Line Draw (or CTRL+F3)

Draws boxes, graphs, and other pictures onscreen when you use the arrow keys. This feature operates in Typeover mode and will not work with a proportionally spaced font.

From the Line Draw menu, you can draw with various characters, including a single line (option 1), a double line (option 2), an asterisk (option 3), or various shaded boxes of different heights and widths (option 4). You also can erase lines you have drawn (option 5) or move the cursor without drawing (option 6).

LINE FORMAT

See FORMAT

LINE HEIGHT

Choose Layout (SHIFT+F8)
Line, Line Height
Auto or Fixed

Sets the amount of vertical space allotted for each line when printed. The line height is determined by

WordPerfect based on the printer that will be used to print your document. When set to Auto, the assumed line height is used but will be adjusted whenever a font or font attribute change alters the size of the characters to be printed. When set to Fixed, line height remains evenly spaced regardless of the font or font attribute you are using. (See also LEADING to add additional space between lines.)

For the Auto menu item, WordPerfect automatically sets the line height to the printer's assumed setting. For the Fixed menu item, WordPerfect displays the assumed line height setting; press ENTER to accept that suggestion, or enter a different line height setting.

LINE NUMBERING

Choose Layout (SHIFT+F8)
Line, Line Numbering

Turns line numbering on or off. With line numbering on, line numbers are inserted near the left margin when the document is printed. Line numbering does not appear in the document window in text mode. It is useful for reference purposes when calling attention to specific line numbers in a document.

LINE SPACING

Choose Layout (SHIFT+F8)
Line, Line Spacing

Alters the spacing between lines of text. The line spacing number is multiplied by the line height to determine the new line spacing. (See also LINE HEIGHT.) WordPerfect displays onscreen the line spacing in whole-number increments only.

Enter a new line spacing number, such as 1/2 or 0.5 for half spacing, 1 for single spacing, and so on. Some printers can even support fractional line spacing, such as 1.3 line spacing.

LISTS

Lets you generate lists of figures, tables, and illustrations in your document.

Defining Lists

Choose Tools (or SHIFT+F8)
List, Define
Create
Type the name of the list, press ENTER
Modify the options in the Create List
   dialog box

Defines the location and page numbering style of the list when it is generated. You can define up to ten lists in each document.

Generating Lists

Generates a list after you have marked the text for the list and defined the list. (See GENERATE CROSS-REFERENCES, INDEXES, LISTS, AND TABLES for the command sequence.)

Marking Text For Lists

Block the text
Choose Tools (or SHIFT+F8)
List, Mark
Enter list name

Marks a word or phrase you wish to be included in a list when generated.

LOCATION OF FILES

Choose File, Setup (or SHIFT+F1)
Location of Files

Indicates to WordPerfect where certain program and document files are stored. Useful if you wish to organize your files on disk such that these other files are stored in separate directories. The options are as follows:

- Backup directory: Specifies the drive or directory where the timed backup files WP{WP}.BK# (where # represents the number of the document window that was backed up at the timed interval) will be stored. (See also BACKUP.)

- Macros/Keyboards/Button Bar: Specifies the drive or directory where all keyboard definitions (ending with the extension .WPK) and all macros (ending with the extension .WPM) and Button Bar definitions are stored. (See also BUTTON BAR, MACROS, and KEYBOARD LAYOUT.)

- Writing Tools: Specifies the drive or directory where the dictionary, spelling, grammar, and thesaurus files are located.

- Printer files: Specifies the drive or directory where the files that contain the printer drivers (files with the extension .ALL or .PRS) are stored. (See also PRINTER, SELECT.)

- Style files: Specifies the drive or directory where the styles files are stored (see also STYLES).

- Graphic files: Specifies the drive or directory where files containing clip art images (such as files with the extension .WPG) are stored.

- Documents: Specifies the default drive or directory for documents that WordPerfect will assume at the start of every working session. The default is the location where files are retrieved from or stored to. (See also DE-

FAULT DRIVE/DIRECTORY, CHANGE for the procedure to change the default in a working session.)

- Spreadsheet files: Specifies the default drive or directory for spreadsheet files for linking operations.

- Quickfinder files: Specifies the default drive or directory for Quickfinder index files.

- WP.DRS File and *.WFW Files: Specifies the default drive or directory for resource files used to support Print Preview and the printing of graphics characters.

- Graphics Fonts Data Files: Specifies the default drive or directory for screen fonts.

- Update Quicklist: Allows you to update the Quicklist so that changes in Location of Files will be reflected in the Quicklist.

LOOK

File, File Manager
Type drive or directory name and press ENTER
Position cursor on a filename
Look

Shows the contents of a file on disk without disrupting the document currently in the active document window. The text is displayed, but not the WordPerfect format of that file.

If a document summary exists for the file (see SUMMARY, DOCUMENT), the summary is displayed first. Select from the menu items at the bottom of the screen or press the DOWN ARROW key to see the text of the file. Use the cursor movement keys to move up and down through the text of the file. Use the Search feature to move the cursor to a specific section of text (see SEARCH), or select from the other menu items at the bottom of the screen to look at the contents of the next or previous document. You cannot edit a document in the Look screen.

MACROS

Creating Macros

Choose Tools, Macro, Record (or CTRL+F10)
Indicate macro name
Perform keystrokes to be recorded
Choose Tools, Macro, Stop (or CTRL+F10)

Records a macro, where a macro is a sequence of
keystrokes that WordPerfect memorizes and can execute
at your command. Give a macro a name with one to eight
letters or with the ALT key plus a letter; WordPerfect
adds the extension .WPM to the filename when stored on
disk. You can name the default macro (sometimes called
a temporary macro) by pressing the ENTER key instead of
typing a name; the macro is stored with the name
WP{WPC}.WPM.

If you need to insert a macro programming command or a
system variable during the recording process, press
CTRL+PGUP and type c. A list of macro commands will be
made available to you. Highlight the desired command or
variable, then choose Insert. You will not be able to see
the macro command/variable on the screen during the
recording process. If you want to check whether it was
inserted, after saving the macro, edit it to see the
commands.

During the macro recording process you cannot use the
mouse for positioning the cursor; you must use the
keyboard.

Drive/Directory Location

Determines where on disk macro files (with the file
extension .WPM) are stored (see LOCATION OF FILES).

Editing Macros

Choose Tools, Macro, Record (or CTRL+F10)
Enter previously created macro name

Choose OK
<u>E</u>dit

Allows you to modify the contents of the macro file. You
can add or delete keystrokes and text and add Macro
Programming commands. (You can edit all macros except
the default macro, which is named with the ENTER key.)

On the Macro Action screen, use the standard typing and
editing keys to delete or insert characters. To insert
editing keystrokes as part of the macro, press SHIFT+F3
to begin recording, perform the needed keystrokes, and
press SHIFT+F3 again to return to editing mode. You can
also type the editing keystroke commands.

Whenever you work with a WordPerfect macro, whether
you are recording or editing, you have access to the
Macro Programming Language. With this language, all
the sophistication of programming is possible for macros.
Press CTRL+PGUP to display a list of programming
language commands. To insert a command, move the
cursor on that command and choose Insert; the command
is inserted in the macro wherever your cursor was
located before you pressed CTRL+PGUP. To leave the
Macro Programming Language commands without
inserting a command, choose Cancel.

Executing Macros

Named with ALT key	ALT+Letter
Otherwise	<u>T</u>ools, <u>M</u>acro, <u>P</u>lay (or CTRL+F10)
	Type macro name and choose OK

Invokes a macro. You can also assign a macro to a key as
part of a keyboard definition. In that case, you can
execute the macro once the keyboard definition has been
selected by pressing the corresponding key (see
KEYBOARD LAYOUT).

Predefined Macros

- ALLFONTS.WPM: Prints names of all fonts for the currently selected printer in their respective typefaces.

- BULLET.WPM: Places a bullet in front of the current paragraph or all of the paragraphs in a block; assigned to ALT+B on the Macros keyboard.

- CALC.WPM: Provides a calculator with Normal and Reverse Polish Notation support; assigned to ALT+C on the Macros keyboard.

- EXITALL.WPM: Moves you from whatever dialog box or substructure you are located in back to the main menu.

- INITCAPS.WPM: Capitalizes the first letter of the current word; assigned to ALT+I on the Macros keyboard.

- MEMO.WPM: Creates memos, letters, and fax cover sheets; assigned to ALT+M on the Macros keyboard.

- MOD_ATRIB.WPM: Replace or add font attributes; assigned to ALT+R on the Macros keyboard.

- NOTECVT.WPM: Converts footnotes to endnotes and vice versa; assigned to ALT+N on the Macros keyboard.

- PLEADING.WPM: Creates legal pleading paper; assigned to ALT+P on the Macros keyboard.

- SPACETAB.WPM: Converts spaces to tabs; assigned to ALT+S on the Macros keyboard.

Replacing Macros

Choose Tools, Macro, Record (or CTRL+F10)
Enter previously created macro name
Choose OK
Replace

Overwrites the existing macro with a new macro that you define.

Setting Options

Tools, Macro, Control (or CTRL+PGUP)
Assign Variable, Macro Record Paused, Macro
   Record Document, Record Abbreviations,
   or Macro Commands

Inserts a special macro command within a macro. Press
CTRL+PGUP while defining a macro wherever you wish
the special macro option to take effect. The five options
are

- Assign Variable: Allows you to create and assign a
  value to a variable, which is useful for when you are creating a sophisticated macro using the Macro Programming Language. When WordPerfect prompts "Variable:",
  type a number from 0 to 9. When WordPerfect prompts
  "Value:", type in the value that you wish to assign.

- Macro Record Paused: Allows you to temporarily pause
  the recording of the macro.

- Macro Record Document: Allows you to switch into record mode if you opened a macro file into a document
  window for editing purposes (by using File, Open instead of Tools, Macro, Edit).

- Record Abbreviations: Macro commands are usually
  stored with long names. Choose this option to store
  shorter names, which will save disk space. For example,
  PageNumberDisplayFormat becomes PgNumDispFmt.

- Macro Commands: Powerful macro programming commands that can incorporate the values of system, global,
  and local variables and evaluate conditional statements.

MAILING LABELS

See LABELS

MARGIN RELEASE

See INDENT

MARGINS

Choose Layout (or SHIFT+F8)
Margins
For Document Margins: Left, Right, Top, Bottom
For Paragraph Margins: Left Margin Adjustment, Right Margin
 Adjustment, First Line Indent, Paragraph Spacing

Changes the margins for entire pages of a document or
for a few paragraphs only. The Paragraph Margin feature
is used only for small numbers of paragraphs within a
document. To change the left or right margins, indent the
first line by a specific amount, or adjust the blank space
between paragraphs. You can also block text before
changing paragraph margins.

MARK FILES

Choose File, File Manager (or F5)
Type drive or directory name
Choose OK
Position cursor on a filename
Type asterisk (*)

Marks specific files with an asterisk in the File Manager
dialog box, so that an operation such as deleting,
printing, moving, copying, or using the Find feature can
be performed on many files at once.

The asterisk acts like a toggle switch; press it once to
mark the highlighted file and press it again to unmark
the file. You can mark all files in the File Manager if none

are marked by pressing ALT+F5 or HOME, *. If some files are marked, press ALT+F5 or HOME, * to unmark all files.

After specific files are marked and you select an option on the List Files menu, a WordPerfect prompt asks whether it is the marked files on which you wish to perform the command. Press Y to perform the command on all the marked files, or N to perform the command on the highlighted file only.

MARK TEXT

Marks text for use with special WordPerfect features (see CROSS-REFERENCE, MASTER DOCUMENTS, INDEXES, TABLES OF AUTHORITIES, TABLES OF CONTENTS, and LISTS).

MASTER DOCUMENTS

Allows for efficient editing and management of long documents. Separate parts of a long document are stored in individual files, called subdocuments, and are linked together in proper order via the master document. This is useful for books that contain numerous chapters or for reports that contain many sections.

Creating a Link to a Subdocument

Position cursor in master where subdocument
    is to be located
Choose File, Master Document
Subdocument
Type name of subdocument, including drive
    and directory

WordPerfect marks the subdocument location onscreen by displaying a comment in a single-line box that reads "Subdoc:" and lists the subdocument filename. To print the complete document, including the master and all subdocuments, expand the master document.

Expanding/Condensing a Master Document

Master document must be onscreen
Choose File, Master Document
Expand or Condense
Use asterisk to mark/unmark files to be expanded/condensed

Expands a master document so you can review and edit the text of the master and all subdocuments at once or print the text in its entirety. Condenses a master document into its original short form before saving the master again to disk.

Before expanding a master document, make sure that all subdocuments have been typed and stored on disk. If, when expanding, WordPerfect cannot locate the name of a subdocument listed in the master, it prompts with a "Subdocument not found" dialog box. Choose Skip to continue the expansion, New Filename to retry the expansion with a new or corrected name, or Cancel to abort the expansion. Once expanded, the document's numbering and option codes for features such as cross-references, footnotes, endnotes, and page numbers remain consecutively numbered and consistent throughout the text.

MATH COLUMNS

Calculating Math Columns

Choose Tools, Math, Calculate

Calculates the results for any math operators placed in the math columns. You can only calculate in that portion of a document where Math has been turned on.

Calculate your math columns as a last step after defining
your columns (if necessary), turning Math on, typing in
numbers and math operators so that they are aligned on
tab stops, and turning Math off.

Position the cursor between the Math On and Math Off
codes before beginning this command sequence.

See TABLES for the procedure to calculate within tables.

Defining Math Columns

Choose Tools, Math, Define
Modify options in the Math dialog box

Defines your math column layout, the first basic step to
creating columns if you wish to calculate down columns
while changing the default math column settings or to
calculate across columns. (Defining columns is generally
unnecessary if you wish to perform simple addition down
columns.) You may wish to change tab stop locations
before defining your column layout.

In the Math dialog box, you define from 2 to 24 columns,
specifying the following:

- Type of columns (numeric, total, text, or calculation)

- How negative numbers are displayed

- Number of digits to the right of the decimal in calculated results

- Formulas for calculation columns

You can only define columns where Math is turned off.

For a calculation column, you must define a math formula
on the Math Definition screen, using the following
symbols when writing the formula:

+	Addition
−	Subtraction
*	Multiplication
/	Division

You also can insert the following special formulas on their own:

+	Add all numeric columns
+/	Average of all numeric columns
=	Add all total columns
=/	Average of all total columns

Inserting Operators

Press TAB until at correct tab stop
Type in a math operator

Inserts a math operator at the location where you want a calculation to occur. (The math operator is a nonprinting character. It will be displayed in the document window, but not on your printed document.) Type math operators only after Math has been turned on. A math operator must be aligned on a tab stop to operate properly. The math operator you insert depends on the calculation you desire:

+	Subtotal
=	Total
*	Grand total

Or, type t in front of a known subtotal, **T** in front of a known total, or **N** in front of a calculated total that you want treated as negative.

If a math column has been defined as a calculation column, when you press TAB to move to that column, WordPerfect inserts the math operator ! on its own, signifying that the result will display in that location after the math columns are calculated.

Turning Math On/Off

COLUMNS/TABLES (ALT+F7) key
Math (3 or M)
On (1 or O) or Off (2 or F)

Turns the Math feature on or off. Turn on Math after defining math columns but before typing numbers and math operators into the math columns. Turn off Math below the math columns. The Math On and Math Off codes that are inserted mark the start and end of the math portion of the document, like bookends.

MAXIMIZE WINDOW

See WINDOWS

MENU BAR

See PULL-DOWN MENUS and "General Reminders" section

MERGE

Lets you combine a form file with a data file or with input from the keyboard to create personalized documents such as letters for mass mailings, envelopes, labels, phone lists, and inventory lists.

Creating a Data (Table) File

Choose Tools, Merge, Define (or SHIFT+F9)
Data [Table]
Create a Table with Field Names
Type first field name (for example, "First Name")
   Press ENTER; repeat operation until all field
   names have been created

Creates a data table file for a merge with a form file. (The alternative is to create a data text file for a merge with a form file.) You will be presented with a table with the field names appearing in the first row. Use TAB and

SHIFT+TAB to navigate in the table. After you finish the first record, when you press the TAB key, another row will be created for you. When you complete the records, save and exit the file.

Creating a Data (Text) Merge Document

Choose Tools, Merge, Define (or SHIFT+F9)
Data [Text]

Establishes a data text file for a merge with a form file. (The alternative is to create a data table file for a merge with a form file.) When you perform this command sequence, it will appear as if nothing has happened, however, you have just instructed WordPerfect to treat the current document as a data text file. The next time you perform the command sequence, you will be presented with the Merge Codes dialog box, from which you can choose the appropriate codes for the operation you are performing.

The data text file contains the variable information (usually an address list) that will be used with a form to produce a personalized document. Separate the record information into fields. For example, in a mailing list, separate one record (name and address of one person) into smaller components such as first name, last name, street address, city, state, and zip code.

Type the information for the first record, one field at a time. At the end of each field, insert an ENDFIELD command by choosing Tools, Merge, Define, End Field (F9). At the end of the record (all of the information for one individual on the mailing list) insert an ENDRECORD code with Tools, Merge, Define, End Record. When you complete the records, save and exit the file.

Creating the Form Document

Choose Tools, Merge, Define (or SHIFT+F9)
Form

Creates a file containing the text that stays the same for each personalized document as well as FIELD and other merge codes that occupy the space where variable inpformation will be inserted during the merge.

Type until you reach the point where field information should be inserted. Then choose Tools, Merge, Define (or SHIFT+F9). Choose Field. Now, type the name of the field. Or, you can choose List Field Names (F5), type the name of the data file, choose OK, and then highlight the field name you need and choose OK. Continue typing the form file, adding FIELD codes where appropriate. You can also add other codes, such as the KEYBOARD merge code, to pause during the merge for you to insert information from the keyboard. When you complete the form, save and exit the file.

When the merge is run, the form file is combined with information from a data file, if FIELD codes are included in the form file, and/or with information typed from the keyboard, if KEYBOARD codes are included.

Merge Codes

FIELD*n*~ During a merge, inserts the variable information contained in the corresponding field in the form file.

ENDRECORD Marks the end of a record in a data file and is followed by a hard page break.

KEYBOARD*message*~ Indicates the location for a pause for input. The message is displayed onscreen during the pause. Press F9 after typing the input.

PAGEOFF Inhibits WordPerfect from placing hard page breaks in the text after each record in the data file is merged with the form file.

NEXTRECORD Causes the merge to continue with the next record in the secondary file.

Advanced merge code commands are also available for enhancing the merge process. To insert one of these commands, select the Merge Codes option in the Merge Codes (Form File) dialog box to display a list of the commands, move the cursor on the command that you wish to select, and press ENTER. Many of the advanced merge code commands have counterparts in the Macro Programming Language (see MACROS).

Running a Merge

Choose Tools, Merge, Run (or CTRL+F9, Merge)
Enter name of the form document (include drive
   and directory names, if necessary)
Enter name of the data file (include drive
   and directory names, if necessary)
Select the Output option if desired
Select Data File and other options if desired
Choose Merge

This initiates a merge process. One of the data file options is Data Record Selection, which lets you mark records or specify conditions under which only certain records should be merged.

During the merge, when the form file contains KEYBOARD merge codes, WordPerfect will pause; type input from the keyboard and press F9 to continue the merge.

After the merge is complete, the cursor is at the bottom of the last merged document if you chose Current Document or Unused Document as the output option. Move the cursor to the top of the file that is on the screen to review, starting with the first merged document.

Setting Field Delimiters

Choose File, Setup (or SHIFT+F1)
Environment
Delimited Text Options

Specifies how fields and records are separated in a DOS text file that will be used as your data file during a merge. To insert codes, choose Codes (F5). A list of codes will be displayed. Highlight the correct code (for example, Carriage Return) and press ENTER. When you are finished inserting codes, choose OK.

MINIMIZE WINDOW

See WINDOWS

MOUSE

For Activating Features and Moving the Cursor

See the "General Reminders" section.

For Marking a Block

Position mouse pointer at one end of the text
Press left mouse button and drag mouse pointer to
    opposite end of the text
Release left mouse button

Marks off (highlights) a portion of a document on which various commands can be performed. The message "Block on" flashes on the screen. See also BLOCK and DRAG AND DROP.

Setting up the Mouse

Choose File, Setup (or SHIFT+F1)
Mouse

Defines the mouse type connected to your computer and how the mouse will operate in WordPerfect, including

- Mouse type and port: The type of mouse (both the brand of mouse and whether it is serial or bus type) attached to your computer and the port (cable connector) at the back of the computer to which it is attached.

- Double-click interval: The interval for double-clicking, measured in 100ths of a second. If two clicks are not pressed within the specified interval, WordPerfect considers the movement as two single clicks rather than as a double-click.

- Acceleration factor: The responsiveness of the mouse pointer onscreen to movements of the mouse, where a greater acceleration factor means a more responsive mouse pointer.

- Left-handed mouse: Whether you will use the mouse with your left hand, so that the tasks performed by the right mouse button can be switched to the left mouse button and vice versa.

MOVE TEXT

See CUT, CUT AND PASTE, and DRAG AND DROP

MOVE/RENAME FILES

File, File Manager (or F5)
Type drive or directory name and press ENTER
Position cursor on a file
Move/Rename

Moves a selected file to another location or changes the filename. Useful if you desire to move a file to a more appropriate directory or provide a document with a more descriptive filename.

When WordPerfect prompts "New name:" with the drive or directory and name of the file, edit the prompt. If you change the drive or directory designation, the file is moved for you. If you change the filename, the file is renamed.

You can move two or more files in one command by marking the files you wish to move with an asterisk before selecting Move/Rename (see MARK FILES).

MULTIPLE COPIES

Choose File, Print/Fax (or SHIFT+F7)
Generated by

Works together with the Number of Copies option. It specifies who controls the number of copies of your text that are printed: WordPerfect or your printer. If WordPerfect controls the print job, you will get collated print jobs.

NEW DOCUMENT

Choose File, New

Opens a new, blank document window. Up to nine document windows can be open at once, depending on the memory limitations of your computer.

NEW PAGE

See PAGE BREAKS

NUMBER OF COPIES

Choose File, Print/Fax (or SHIFT+F7)
Number of Copies

A print option that can specify the number of copies.
This option is useful for producing multiple copies of a
document in one print job.

NUMBER PAGES

See PAGE NUMBERING

OPEN DOCUMENT

Choose File, Open (or SHIFT+F10)
Type filename including drive and directory name
Choose OK

Opens an existing file into a clear document window for
review, editing, or printing. If the file is locked,
WordPerfect requests a password. See also RETRIEVE
DOCUMENT for another method for recalling a document
to the screen.

Be sure to precede the filename by a path (drive or
directory) if the file is stored in other than the default
document directory.

You can also open a document from the File Manager by
positioning the cursor on a file and choosing Open. See
FILE MANAGER.

OTHER FORMAT

See FORMAT

OUTLINING

Lets you create outline entries in a document, using numbers, letters, bullets, or headings as the outline numbering method.

Beginning/Ending an Outline

Choose Tools, Outline (or CTRL+F5)
Begin New Outline
Highlight desired outline style
Choose Select
Type the outline entries
Choose Tools, Outline (or CTRL+F5)
End Outline

Activates outlining and specifies the numbering style for the outline numbers. You can select from predefined styles or you can select an outline style that you created.

When outlining is active, the keyboard operates as follows to create outlines:

- ENTER inserts a hard return and an outline number.

- TAB moves the outline number to the next tab stop and changes the outline number to the next level.

- SHIFT+TAB moves the outline number to the previous tab stop and changes the outline number to the previous level.

After turning off outlining, you can return to standard typing.

Displaying/Hiding the Outline Bar

Choose View, Outline Bar

Offers quick access to many of the outline options. Used with a mouse. To make the mnemonic characters on the outline bar available for use with a keyboard, press

CTRL+O, which turns on Outline Edit. Press CTRL+O again to turn off edit mode.

Modifying Outline Styles

Choose Tools, Outline (or CTRL+F5)
Outline Styles

Lets you create or edit an outline style. You can change the format for the outline numbers, the numbering for each level, and a new style for each level.

Move/Copy/Deleting Outline Families

Place the cursor on the first line of the family
Choose Tools, Outline (or CTRL+F5)
Move Family, Copy Family, Cut Family,
    or Paste

Moves, copies, or deletes an entire outline family, where an outline family is the outline level on the line where the cursor is located plus any lower levels.

WordPerfect highlights the outline family in reverse video. For moving, use the arrow keys to reposition the outline family and press ENTER. For copying, use the arrow keys to reposition the copy of the outline family that is created and press ENTER. To paste a previously cut or copied family, move the cursor to the new location, then paste.

Showing/Hiding Outline Families

Place cursor in the first line of the family below which
    the levels are to be hidden
Choose Tools, Outline (or CTRL+F5)
Hide Family or Show Family

Collapses the outline, hiding all lower levels. Or, expands the outline, revealing the levels that had been hidden.

OVERSTRIKE

Choose Layout (or SHIFT+F8)
Character
Create Overstrike or Edit Overstrike

Prints two or more characters in the same position.
Useful for inserting in a document special characters
such as ö or è, which may not print on your printer with
the Compose feature (see COMPOSE). The result is
shown on the printed page; in text mode, only the last
character will be displayed.

For the Create menu item, enter the characters that will
print where the cursor is located. For the Edit menu item,
position the cursor forward from the overstrike you wish
to alter before following the key sequence; the overstrike
characters will appear for editing.

PAGE BREAKS

Inserting Hard Page Breaks

Layout, Alignment, Hard Page (or CTRL+ENTER)

Starts the cursor at the top of a new page, which is
useful when you wish to end a short page of text,
controlling where a page break will be. Also used to end
a column and start a new one when working in text
columns.

A page bar (a double line) across the document window
indicates the page break. The status line also reflects the
change in page number.

Inserting Soft Page Breaks

No command sequence; performed by WordPerfect

Starts the cursor at the top of a new page after you type
a complete page of text, determined by WordPerfect
based on settings for top and bottom margins (see
MARGINS) and page length (see PAPER SIZE/TYPE).

A page bar (a single line) across the editing screen
indicates the page break. The status line reflects the
change in page number. This page bar will readjust if
text is later edited.

PAGE MODE

See the "General Reminders" section

PAGE NUMBERING

Formatting Page Numbers

Choose Layout (or SHIFT+F8)
Page, Page Numbering, Page Number Format

Specifies the format for the page number when you turn
on page numbering or insert the page number in a
specific document. Text and Secondary Page, Chapter
and Volume number codes can be included in the page
number style. To include text with the page number,
position the cursor either before or after the [Page #]
code in the Page Number Format entry field, then type.
To include Secondary Page, Chapter and Volume number
codes, position the cursor in the entry field, then choose
Number Codes (F5), select the code, and press ENTER.

Inserting Page Numbers in Text

Choose Layout (or SHIFT+F8)
Page
Page Numbering
Insert Formatted Page Number

Inserts the page number at the cursor location in the current page number style.

Positioning Page Numbers

Choose Layout (or SHIFT+F8)
Page, Page Numbering, Page Number Position

Turns on page numbering and selects the position where the page numbers will print, or turns off page numbering. Make sure that the cursor is on the appropriate page before initiating this feature. The page numbers appear on the printed page, but not in the document window when working in text and graphics modes. Page numbers are displayed on the screen when working in page mode.

There are nine options to choose from when selecting where to print page numbers: 1) top left, 2) top center, 3) top right, 4) alternating top, 5) bottom left, 6) bottom center, 7) bottom right, 8) alternating bottom, or 9) no page numbering. (See SUPPRESS FOR CURRENT PAGE for the procedure to suppress page numbering for a specific page in a document.)

Renumbering Pages

Choose Layout (or SHIFT+F8)
Page, Page Numbering, Page Number, New Number

Renumbers all pages starting on the page where your cursor was located before you performed the command sequence. Make sure that the cursor is on the page where the new numbering should begin before initiating this feature.

Setting Numbering Method

Choose Layout (or SHIFT+F8)
Page, Page Numbering, Page Number, Numbering Method

Five numbering methods are available: Number (1, 2, 3), Lower Letters (a, b, c), Upper Letters, (A, B, C), Lower Roman (i, ii, iii) and Upper Roman (I, II, III).

PAPER DEFINITIONS

Contains information WordPerfect requires to print your text, such as the paper type, paper size, and location of the paper. During printing, WordPerfect uses this information whenever it encounters a paper size/type code in the document (see PAPER SIZE/TYPE) that specifies a particular paper definition.

Adding Paper Definitions

Choose Layout (or SHIFT+F8)
Page, Paper Size/Type, Create

Creates a new paper definition for the currently selected printer. In the Create Paper Size/Type dialog box, begin by giving the new paper definition a name. Then define the paper's characteristics, including the following:

- Paper Type: The type of paper (choose "Other" if none of the listed types apply).

- Paper Size: The size (dimensions) of the paper. If the dimensions you specify do not meet the requirements of the printer (too short for the printer's paper path, for instance), WordPerfect will automatically adjust the dimensions to the minimum or maximum allowable.

- Paper Location: The whereabouts of the paper during printing. The options available depend on the currently selected printer. At a minimum, you should be able to specify either Continuous (from one continuous form feeder, such as a paper tray, or using continuous-feed paper) and Manual. If the printer you have selected (through the Print menu) has a sheet feeder or optional paper cassettes (such as an envelope feeder), you will see those options in the Location of Paper dialog box.

- Prompt to Load: Whether WordPerfect should pause before printing. If set to No, this implies that the paper is available in the printer. If set to Yes, WordPerfect will sound a beep so that you can insert paper; then select

Go from the Control Printer dialog box to start the printing. (See also CONTROL PRINTER.)

- Orientation: The orientation of fonts used for printing, pertinent only for printers in which paper cannot be inserted sideways. For instance, a landscape font type is used in laser printers for printing out an address on an envelope. Portrait orientation means that the paper is taller than it is wide, and landscape orientation means that the paper is wider than it is tall. At the printer level, orientation is controlled either by using a font that is specifically designed to print in portrait or landscape orientation or, if the printer has this capability, rotating the fonts to portrait or landscape orientation.

- Text Adjustment: The page offsets that are necessary to compensate for paper that is loaded into the printer at different horizontal or vertical positions than what Word-Perfect assumes.

Managing Paper Definitions

Choose Layout (or SHIFT+F8)
Page
Paper Size/Type
Edit or Delete

Allows you to manipulate existing paper definitions. You can edit or delete a definition by positioning the cursor on the paper definition and selecting the appropriate menu item. For a deletion, choose Yes to verify.

PAPER SIZE/TYPE

Choose Layout (or SHIFT+F8)
Page
Paper Size/Type
Highlight the desired paper type
Select

Indicates to WordPerfect which preexisting paper definition should be used to print out all or part of a document (see also PAPER DEFINITIONS). Text will adjust onscreen if the selected paper definition results in a change in paper size. When changing paper size, you may find that a modification in margins is also warranted.

The cursor can be positioned on a paper definition that you wish to select either by using the arrow keys or by pressing N to initiate the Name Search feature, then typing the first letters of the paper type for that paper definition, and pressing ENTER. Select "[ALL OTHERS]" and indicate a size and type for paper without a previously defined definition and for which you do not wish to create a new paper definition.

PARAGRAPH NUMBERING

Defining Numbering Style and Starting Number

See OUTLINING

Inserting Paragraph Number

Choose Tools, Outline, Outline Options (or CTRL+F5)
Insert Outline Level (1-8)
Type number for desired level

Inserts a paragraph number on the line where the cursor is located. The location of the paragraph number in relation to the tab stop is determined by the outline level. When you press ENTER, a new number will appear on the next line. When you press TAB or SHIFT+TAB, a new level will be selected.

If you want to control when a new number will be inserted in the document instead of relying on the automatic method, you will have to modify the outline style (Tools, Outline, Outline Options, Outline Style, highlight desired style, choose Edit, Numbers Only).

PASSWORD

Locking Files

Choose File, Save As (or F10)
Enter a filename
Password (or F8)
Type password and press ENTER
Type the password again to confirm, press ENTER

Locks a file so that its contents cannot be opened, looked at, or printed (even in other programs) without use of the proper password. Useful for ensuring that a document on disk remains confidential. You must remember the password or you will be locked out of the file.

Enter a password that contains 23 characters or less. When you enter the password, it does not appear onscreen; thus, you enter it twice to make sure you are not making a typing mistake. After adding (or changing) the password, remember to resave the file so that the password is attached to the document permanently (or until you unlock the file).

Unlocking Files

Choose File, Save As (or F10)
Password (F8)
Remove (F6)

Unlocks a previously locked document. After unlocking the file, remember to resave the file so that the password is removed from the document permanently (or until you add a password again).

PITCH

See FONT and WORD AND LETTER SPACING to alter the width of and amount of space between characters on the printed page. *See* DISPLAY PITCH to alter the pitch onscreen.

PREVIEW

See PRINT PREVIEW

PRINT

Lets you print your text on paper. When you issue a print command, a print job is created. See also CONTROL PRINTER for ways to pause or cancel a print job.

Printing a Block from Screen

Block the text
Choose File, Print/Fax (or SHIFT+F7)
Blocked Text
Print (ENTER)

Prints a highlighted block from the screen, which is useful if you wish to print only a portion of a page currently onscreen, such as two paragraphs.

Printing Documents on Disk

Choose File, Print/Fax (or SHIFT+F7)
Document on Disk
Enter filename
Choose OK
Enter page numbers in Print Multiple Pages dialog box
Choose OK

or

Choose File, File Manager (or F5)
Type drive or directory name
Choose OK
Position cursor on a file
Print
Enter page numbers in Print Multiple Pages dialog box
Choose OK

Prints any number of pages of a document from disk.
(See "Printing Documents from Screen," below, for
instructions concerning the use of the Print Multiple
Pages dialog box.)

Printing Documents from Screen

Choose File, Print/Fax (or SHIFT+F7)
Full Document, Page, or Multiple Pages

Prints one of the following for the document currently
onscreen: the full text, including all pages; the page
where the cursor is currently located; or multiple pages.
For multiple pages, in the Print Multiple Pages dialog
box, choose Page/Label Range, Secondary Page(s),
Chapter(s), Volume(s), and/or Odd/Even Pages; enter a
single page number (such as 5), a range of consecutive
pages separated by a hyphen (such as 2-5), or a range of
nonconsecutive pages separated by commas (such as
1,5,7). When printing multiple pages, you can also choose
Document Summary to print the document summary, if
there is one, Print as Booklet, and Descending Order.

PRINT TO DISK

Choose File, Print/Fax (or SHIFT+F7)
Select
Position cursor on printer name
Edit, Port, Filename

Enter filename to be used for document printed to disk
Choose OK

Prints a document to a file on disk. This is useful when
you wish to print the document later with DOS
commands on a printer located where WordPerfect is
unavailable.

Before changing the port setting, make a copy of the
printer definition so that you can have one definition to
print to disk and one to print to the printer. Or, make a
note of its current setting so that you can restore the
information later.

Once you follow the command sequence, return to your
document. Make sure that you select the same printer
name for printing your document as the one for which
you altered the port. Print the document from the screen.

PRINT OPTIONS

Choose File, Print/Fax (or SHIFT+F7)
Setup (or SHIFT+F1)

Alters the default print options assumed for printing out
documents for the currently selected printer, which
WordPerfect Corporation sets up to include the following:

Number of Copies	1
Multiple Copies Generated by	WordPerfect
Text Quality	High
Graphics Quality	Medium
Print Color	Full Color
Redline Method	Printer Dependent
Baseline Placement for Typesetter (First Baseline at Top Margin)	Off

Graphical Printing of HP Laserjet   24
Fonts; Threshold Point Size

When you change any of these print options in the Print
Setup dialog box, the new settings remain as the default
settings for each subsequent use of WordPerfect.

See also BINDING OFFSET, MULTIPLE COPIES, NUMBER
OF COPIES, REDLINE, and TEXT/GRAPHICS QUALITY to
learn how to alter those print options settings for print
jobs in only the current working session.

PRINT PREVIEW

Choose File, Print Preview
or
Choose File, Print/Fax (or SHIFT+F7)
Preview

Lets you preview how your document will look when
printed. Choose items from the Preview menu bar or
from the Button Bar. You can see one or two full pages at
a time, or zoom in for detail on a section of the page.

PRINTER COMMANDS

Position cursor in document at the location
    where special command should take control
Choose Layout, Printer Functions, Printer Command
Type the command in the entry field or type the
    name of the file that contains the printer instructions
Choose OK

Occasionally, you may need to print a document using
special printer features to which WordPerfect does not
provide access. You will have to provide instructions
(usually called "escape codes") to the printer via the

Printer Commands dialog box. Printer commands are usually entered in decimal ASCII, as provided in the printer manual. Decimal codes less than 32 and greater than 126 must be entered in angle brackets, such as <15>. Consult your printer documentation for the correct commands and syntax.

PRINTER CONTROL

See CONTROL PRINTER

PRINTER DEFINITIONS

Creating Printer Definitions

Choose File, Print/Fax (or SHIFT+F7)
Select
Add Printer
Position cursor on printer for which you wish
  to create a definition
Select
Enter a filename for the printer file stored on disk or
  choose OK to accept WordPerfect's suggestion
Read over the Helps and Hints screen for that printer
Choose Close
Make any desired changes in the Edit Printer Setup
  dialog box (see "Editing/Managing Printer Definitions")
Choose OK
Select (If printer should become the new default)

Creates a printer definition (with the extension .PRS) that will be used to select a printer and print out your documents. Select Other Dir if, after selecting the Add Printers menu item, the name of your printer does not appear. In the Add Printer dialog box, type in the drive or directory where other (previously installed) printer files (with an extension .ALL) are stored. Then continue with the command sequence shown. (To display more printers, you must run the Installation program and install additional printer files.)

Editing/Managing Printer Definitions

Choose File, Print/Fax (or SHIFT+F7)
Select
Highlight printer definition
Edit, Delete, Copy, Information or Update

Allows you to manipulate existing printer definitions. Edit, copy, or delete a printer definition, or use the Information option to display a Helps and Hints screen for that printer and sheet feeder. Or use the Update option to upgrade a printer definition for changes. When editing, you can alter any of the following printer settings that are incorrect:

- Description: Name that appears on the Print screen next to the item "Select Printer". A name can be up to 36 characters in length and can contain spaces.

- Port: Port (plug) where the printer is attached. LPT represents a parallel port, while COM represents a serial port.

- Network Port: This option is only available if WordPerfect is installed on a Network. Specifies the location for print jobs controlled by a network operating system such as NOVELL. If you are on a NOVELL 3.11 system, you can direct print jobs to a print queue using the convention /[servername]/[devicename]. If you are not using a NOVELL operating system, but have print queue capability, WordPerfect may be able to direct print jobs to a queue using the Universal Naming Convention //[servername]/[devicename]. If this does not work, check your network operating system documentation for the procedure to capture or redirect print jobs to a print queue.

- Printer Configured for Color: Only available if your printer has color printing capability.

- Sheet Feeder: Sheet feeder that is used to feed paper into your printer. If you use no sheet feeder, leave this option set to No sheet feeder defined.

- Cartridges and Fonts: The fonts and cartridges you will use with your printer (see also CAR-TRIDGES/FONTS/PRINTWHEELS).

- Font Setup: All default font settings including initial font, cartridges/fonts/printwheels, automatic font changes, font mapping tables, and size ratios (see also FONT).

- Directory for Soft Fonts: The drive and/or directory where files for downloadable fonts are stored (see also DOWNLOADABLE (SOFT) FONTS).

PRINTER, SELECT

Choose File, Print/Fax (or SHIFT+F7)
Select
Highlight desired printer
Select

Determines which printer among the printers that you previously defined will print the document onscreen (see also PRINTER DEFINITIONS). If you defined only one printer, that printer is your only option.

Once a document is saved, the current printer selection is saved with the document (unless you have Fast Save enabled). The next time you retrieve or print that document from disk, WordPerfect formats that document for the saved printer selection.

PROPORTIONAL SPACING

Proportional spacing alters the way in which characters are spaced, so that characters occupy an amount of space proportional to their width. This can give a document a more professional look. If your printer supports proportional spacing, then you activate it by the font that you select to print out your document. (See FONT for the command sequence to select a font.)

PULL-DOWN MENUS

Choose View, Pull-down Menus

Displays/hides the pull-down menu bar. When the menu bar is hidden, click the right mouse button or press ALT+= to temporarily display it. See also SCREEN SETUP.

QUICKFINDER

Indexes can rapidly scan through a group of documents to create a list of files meeting the word or word pattern criteria you specify. Because Quickfinder uses an index instead of looking at every word in a document, it is much faster than using the Search feature. Also, a Quickfinder index can include documents from various locations.

Quickfinder can index WordPerfect 4.2, 5.0, 5.1, and 6.0 documents. All other file formats will be considered ASCII, and Quickfinder will index their contents as ASCII text.

Creating a Quickfinder Index

Choose File, File Manager (or F5)
Use Quickfinder (or F4)
Setup (or SHIFT+F1, location of FiLes)
Choose Personal Path or Shared Path
Type the path of the directory that will house
    the Quickfinder Index
Choose OK

Create Index Definition
Type a description to identify the group of
   files being indexed
Press ENTER
Modify the proposed index name and press ENTER
   (or simply press ENTER to accept the suggested name)
Add
Type the pathname of the directory containing the
   files to be indexed (you can include a filename
   pattern to restrict the index to certain files
   (for example, C:\WPDOCS*.LET)
Include Subdirectories (only if you wish to index
   files in subdirectories)
Choose OK
To include additional directories, repeat the steps
   from Add to here until all of the
   desired directories have been identified
Options
   Level, Exclude Files, Index Document Text,
   Index Document Summary, Index Both, Index
   WP Documents Only, Include Numbers, Manual
   Update Only
Choose OK, OK
Choose Generate Marked Indexes

WordPerfect will begin indexing the selected directories.
During the indexing procedure, WordPerfect will present
you with a status screen to apprise you of the process.
When the index is completed, you will be brought to the
Quickfinder File Indexer dialog box. You may use the
index at this point or choose Close to return to the
document window.

Editing a Quickfinder Index

Choose File, File Manager (or F5)
Use Quickfinder (or F4)
Setup (or SHIFT+F1)
Highlight the index name

<u>E</u>dit
Add, delete, or edit directories and files that are indexed

Updating Quickfinder Indexes

Choose <u>F</u>ile, <u>F</u>ile Manager (or F5)
Use Quickfinder (or F4)
Press ESC to back out of I<u>n</u>dex option
<u>Up</u>date Indexes

After modifying an index, it is important to update it. Occasionally, you may also want to regenerate an index to recompact it.

Using a Quickfinder Index

Choose <u>F</u>ile, <u>F</u>ile Manager (or F5)
Use Quickfinder (or F4)
Select or enter the name of the desired index
<u>W</u>ord Pattern
Type a word pattern you want to base the search on,
   or if you want to include an operator in the pattern,
   choose Operators (F5) and
   insert the operator in the search string
Choose OK

WordPerfect will perform the search and present you with a list of files matching the word pattern you specified.

QUICKLIST

Choose <u>F</u>ile, <u>F</u>ile Manager (or F5)
Quicklist (or F6)

Lets you use descriptive names for directories and files that you use often. Especially useful when you store files in many directories and/or have numerous levels of

hierarchy on your hard disk (such as
C:\WPDOCS\BUSINESS\LEGAL). Quicklist lets you
avoid typing cumbersome directory paths.

Follow the command sequence above and choose Create
to create Quicklist names and their associated directories
or paths. You can also edit or delete Quicklist names.
WordPerfect predefines some Quicklist names for you.

Take advantage of the Quicklist names whenever you
use a feature that requires you to specify a file or
directory. For instance, when you wish to see the File
Manager for files in the directory that you assigned a
Quicklist name, follow the command sequence above,
highlight the Quicklist name, and choose Select.

REDLINE

See APPEARANCE for the command sequence to insert
redline manually. See DOCUMENT COMPARE for the
command sequence to have WordPerfect compare two
documents and insert redline automatically, where text
in the document onscreen does not appear in the
document on disk.

The redline markings are based on your printer and the
redline method that you select.

Selecting a Method

Choose Layout (or SHIFT+F8)
Document
Redline Method
Printer Dependent, Left, Alternating or Right

Chooses how redline markings will appear on the printed
page. The Printer Dependent menu item marks redlined
text based on your printer's default option. Usually it is
shading that appears over characters. The Left option
marks redlined text with a horizontal bar or another
character in the left margin. Alternating marks redlined

text with a character in the left margin for even-numbered pages and in the right margin for odd-numbered pages. Right marks redlined text with a horizontal bar or another character in the right margin. For those last three options, you must also enter the redline character to be used in the next field in the Document Format dialog box.

REMOVE REDLINE AND STRIKEOUT

Choose <u>F</u>ile, Compare <u>D</u>ocuments
<u>R</u>emove Markings
<u>R</u>emove Redline Markings and Strikeout Text or
    Remove <u>S</u>trikeout Text Only

Removes all the redline markings and all the strikeout text from the entire document onscreen in one command. This is useful to return to the edited version of a document after using the Document Compare feature. Also useful after making revisions using redline and strikeout and then deciding to make those revisions permanent.

Or, when choosing Remove Strikeout Text Only, deletes only strikeout text, but keeps the markings for added text.

REPEAT

CTRL+R
Type number of repetitions
Type character or command

Repeats a specified number of times either a character, a macro, or the following cursor movement and deletion commands:

↑	PGUP
↓	PGDN

←	+ (numeric keypad)
→	- (numeric keypad)
CTRL+←	CTRL+BACKSPACE
CTRL+→	CTRL+END
DEL	CTRL+PGDN

When WordPerfect displays the Repeat dialog box, type in the number of repetitions desired. (The default setting is eight repetitions; if you want eight repetitions, there is no need to type in a number.) Type the character, execute a macro, or type a cursor movement command or a deletion command.

You can also change the default number of repetitions for a working session by pressing CTRL+R, typing a number, and choosing Set.

REPLACE

Choose Edit, Replace (or ALT+F2)
Type the search string
Press ENTER
Type the replace string
Press ENTER
Choose any desired options:
   Confirm Replacement, Backward Search,
   Case Sensitive Search, Find Whole Words
   Only, Extended Search (Hdrs, Ftrs, etc.)
   Limit Number of Matches:
Choose Replace (or F2)

Replaces a search string (word, code, or phrase) with a replace string (another word, code, or phrase), beginning at the cursor position and continuing to the end of the document. This is useful for altering repeated occurrences of text or codes or for deleting certain codes from the text. (Delete codes or text by leaving the replace string empty.)

If you select Confirm Replacement, the program stops to ask for confirmation before replacing each occurrence in the text of the search string; otherwise, the replacement occurs for the entire document in one operation.

To add a code to the search string, choose Codes (F5) and select the desired code to insert it into the search string.

To replace specific codes such as a particular font code, select the search string field, then choose Specific Codes (SHIFT+F5) and select the desired code. WordPerfect will then open the appropriate dialog box to help you specify the correct code.

You can perform the replace on only a portion of a document by blocking text before beginning the command sequence.

RETRIEVE DOCUMENT

Choose File, Retrieve (or SHIFT+F10, SHIFT+F10)
Type filename
Choose OK

Retrieves a copy of a file from disk into the active document window for review, editing, or printing. If there is text in the active document window, the retrieved document will be combined with the existing text. Be sure to precede the filename by a path (drive or directory), if the file is stored in other than the default document directory. See also OPEN DOCUMENT for another method for recalling a document to the screen.

You can also retrieve a document from the File Manager by positioning the cursor on a file and choosing Retrieve. See FILE MANAGER.

RETURN

Inserting Hard Returns

ENTER

Moves the cursor down to the next line of text and is useful to end a short line of text, end a paragraph, or insert a blank line. (See also SCREEN SETUP for the method to specify a character to represent a hard return on the editing screen.)

If a soft return code is followed immediately by a hard return code, the hard return code is changed to a dormant hard return. This eliminates blank lines that appear at the top of a page or column.

Inserting Soft Returns

No key sequence; performed by WordPerfect

Starts the cursor at the beginning of the next line after you type a full line of text. This is known as word wrap. Where word wrap occurs depends on the settings for features such as the left and right margins (see MARGINS) and the page width (see PAPER SIZE/TYPE). The line end will readjust if text is later edited.

REVEAL CODES

Choose View, Reveal Codes (or F11 or ALT+F3)

Splits the screen. The top window shows the text as it appears in the document window. The bottom window shows the same text along with the location of codes in that text. The two windows are separated by a ruler line. It is useful to reveal codes when you wish to determine whether a feature that only takes effect at the printer has been activated or to find the location of a code you wish to delete. You can add or delete both text and codes while viewing the Reveal Codes screen.

To turn off Reveal Codes, perform the same command sequence.

The size of the bottom window on the Reveal Codes screen can be changed; choose View, Screen Setup, Reveal Codes.

REWRITE SCREEN

CTRL+F3
Rewrite

Manually readjusts text onscreen according to current format settings (such as margins). Useful if the screen does not redraw properly after text is edited.

RIBBON

Choose View, Ribbon

Displays or hides the Ribbon. Your choice to display or hide the ribbon has an effect in text mode independent from graphics or page mode. The Ribbon can be used to quickly modify the appearance of your document. When it is displayed on the screen, it is located directly underneath the menu bar. The features on the Ribbon can only be accessed with a mouse.

The Ribbon includes tools for 1) changing the document display size on the screen, 2) changing the paragraph level in an outline, 3) changing the number of columns used in the document, 4) changing the alignment of text, 5) changing the font style, and 6) changing the font size.

SAVE

Choose File, Save (CTRL+F12)

Used to update the document on disk with the modifications on the screen. You will not be prompted to confirm the replacement. If the document has not previously been saved, the SAVE feature will work like the SAVE AS feature.

SAVE AS

Used when you need to give a name to a file before saving it on disk. You can provide a filename for a new document. Or, you can provide a different filename for a document that has previously been saved. In this way, you can save modifications to another file and preserve the original.

Saving Blocked Text

Block the text
Choose File, Save As (or F10)
Type filename
Choose OK

Stores a copy of the highlighted text in a file of its own. This is useful if you wish to store just a part of a document on disk. If a file by that name already exists on disk, WordPerfect asks for confirmation to replace the old version with the new screen version.

Saving Files

Choose File, Save As (or F10)
Type filename

Stores a copy of the screen version of the document on disk. If a file by that name already exists on disk,

WordPerfect asks for confirmation to replace the old
version with the new screen version. Also, if you wish to
save to a drive or directory other than the default,
precede the filename with the other drive or directory
name. After saving, the document remains onscreen.

Saving in Other Format

Choose File, Save As (or F10)
Type filename
Format
Highlight desired format
Press ENTER

Stores a file from the screen to disk in one of 48 formats,
including ASCII and earlier WordPerfect formats.

SCREEN SETUP

View, Screen Setup

Lets you determine the look of elements onscreen. Items
include Screen Options to specify the status of features
such as the pull-down menus, ribbon, and Button Bar;
Display Character to specify the character used to
represent a space or hard return; Display of Merge Codes
to determine whether merge codes are displayed,
displayed as icons, or hidden; Window Options to
determine whether the window is framed and displays
scroll bars; Reveal Codes to determine the size of the
Reveal Codes screen; and Zoom to specify the zoom
magnitude. (You must be in graphics mode to choose the
Zoom option.)

The selections you make will stay in effect as a default
until you change them again. Some of these options can
also be changed on the View menu.

SCROLL BARS

Choose View, Vertical Scroll Bar
or
Choose View, Horizontal Scroll Bar

Lets you display or hide scroll bars. Scroll bars are used with the mouse to move through the text. Each scroll bar has scroll arrows and a scroll box. Click a scroll arrow to move in the corresponding direction. Drag the scroll box to move the proportional amount in the document. For instance, drag the vertical scroll box to the bottom to move to the bottom of the document.

Your choice to display or hide a scroll bar has an effect in text mode independent from graphics or page mode. For instance, display a scroll bar in text mode, and the scroll bar will not display when you switch to graphics (or page) mode. See also SCREEN SETUP.

SEARCH

Choose Edit, Search (or F2)
Type in search string
Press ENTER
Choose options:
   Backward Search, Case Sensitive Search,
   Find Whole Words Only, Extended Search
   (Hdrs, Ftrs, etc.)
Choose Search (or F2)

Positions the cursor just past the next occurrence of the search string (word, code, or phrase) in the text. The forward search checks ahead in the text for the next occurrence, and the reverse search checks backward. This is useful for quickly moving the cursor to a certain title, phrase, or code in the document.

You can extend the Search feature to headers, footers, footnotes, endnotes, graphics box captions, and text boxes by choosing the Extended Search option.

To search backward through the document, choose the Backward Search option.

To add a code to the search string, choose Codes (F5) and select the desired code to insert it into the search string.

To search for a particular code, choose Specific Codes (SHIFT+F5) and select the desired code. WordPerfect will then open the appropriate dialog box to help you construct the correct code.

You can perform the search on only a portion of a document by blocking text before beginning the command sequence.

SELECT

An alternate method for blocking text, when the text is a discrete unit. (See also BLOCK.)

Selecting a Sentence, Paragraph, or Page

Position the cursor in the text
Choose Edit, Select
Sentence, Paragraph, or Page

Marks off (highlights) the sentence, paragraph, or page on which commands can be performed. The message "Block on" appears on the screen.

Selecting a Tabular Column or Rectangle

Block the column or rectangle
Choose Edit, Select
Tabular Column or Rectangle
Delete, Cut and Paste, or Copy and Paste

Lets you delete, cut and paste, or copy and paste a tabular column or rectangle. A tabular column is text or numbers aligned on a tab stop. A rectangle is a rectangular-shaped portion of text, such as two tabular columns, or a square section in a line drawing.

To block the tabular column, start with any character on the first line of the column and end with any character on the last line. The highlighted block will not look like a column until you choose Tabular Column.

To block the rectangle, start with the character in the upper-left corner and end with the character in the lower-right corner. The highlighted block will not look like a column until you choose Rectangle.

SETUP

Choose File, Setup (or SHIFT+F1)

Alters a wide range of options for how WordPerfect operates. A change in any option on the Setup menu remains in effect each time you start WordPerfect and for all *new* documents. This is useful if you wish to tailor the operation of the WordPerfect program for your own special needs. (See also COLORS ON SCREEN, ENVIRONMENT, KEYBOARD LAYOUT, LOCATION OF FILES, and MOUSE.)

The last setup option, Color Printing Palette, lets you select, create, or edit color printing palettes. These palettes categorize colors. You can create and name colors so that you can select them easily. The actual appearance of the colors depends on the capabilities of your printer. To choose from a color palette for printing, see COLORS AT THE PRINTER. Or, there is a color option provided in the dialog box for specific features such as Graphics Lines and Graphics Boxes.

See also INITIAL SETTINGS for information on the initial setup for the formatting in documents.

SHEET FEEDER

Defines the type of sheet feeder used with your printer (see PRINTER DEFINITIONS for the command sequence). You specify the sheet-feeder bin numbers where certain types of paper are located when you define the paper forms that will be used in your printer (see PAPER DEFINITIONS for the command sequence).

SHELL, EXIT TO

Choose File, Go to Shell (or CTRL+F1)
Active Programs, Clipboard, or DOS

If you have the WordPerfect Shell running, the Shell menu allows you to use a clipboard or to exit temporarily to DOS, for example. If Shell is not running, this command sequence only exits you temporarily to DOS (see DOS, EXIT TO).

Use the Active Programs option to switch temporarily to another application program or to Shell. If hot keys (usually CTRL+ALT+Letter) have been assigned to the programs that are run from the Shell, you can use the hot keys to move temporarily from one program to another instead of using the command sequence described above.

Use the Clipboard option to work with one of 80 (0-79) clipboards. Choose the desired clipboard number first, then specify whether you wish to save to, append, or retrieve from the clipboard. The clipboard allows you to transfer text or graphics between different software programs or just within WordPerfect.

To run Shell, you must not be in WordPerfect. (Exit WordPerfect if it is loaded.) At the DOS prompt, type **cd \wpc60dos** and press ENTER to switch to the directory where the WordPerfect Shell program files are stored. (Note that if you or your installer created a directory with a different name to house the Shell files, you will have to substitute the correct directory name after you type **cd** \.) Then type **shell** and press ENTER. The first time you run Shell, you will want to create a menu structure.

SIZE ATTRIBUTE RATIOS

Choose Font, Font (or CTRL+F8)
Setup (or SHIFT+F1)
Size Ratios
Fine, Small, Large, Very Large, Extra Large
   Superscript/Subscript
Type number representing new percentage of
   change for the selected attribute

Determines the size of text controlled by a given size attribute. The default settings as a percentage of the normal font size are Fine = 60%, Small = 80%, Large = 120%, Very Large = 150%, Extra Large = 200%, Super/Subscript = 60%.

SIZE/POSITION

Choose Font (or CTRL+F8)
Size/Position
Normal Size, Fine, Small, Large, Very Large,
   Extra Large, Normal Position, Suprscpt,
   or Subscpt

For the current font, alters the attribute that controls the size of characters at the printer. This feature selects smaller or larger fonts only if they exist for the font, or if the font is *scalable*, meaning that it can be sized. If a larger or smaller font in the same family as the current font is not available, WordPerfect will attempt to make a substitution from another font family. See also SIZE ATTRIBUTE RATIOS.

Or, this feature alters the position of characters, placing them slightly above (superscript) or below (subscript) the standard line of text. This is useful in equations and other statistical typing. WordPerfect uses this feature automatically to print out footnote and endnote reference numbers in the text. Superscript and subscript text will print smaller than the normal size.

To activate a size attribute as you type, follow the command sequence to turn on the desired size attribute. Next, type the text, and then turn off the size attribute either by 1) pressing the RIGHT ARROW key, 2) repeating the same commands you used to turn on the attribute, or 3) by choosing Font, Normal Size or Normal Position, as appropriate.

To activate a size attribute for existing text, use the Block feature to highlight the existing text before following the command sequence.

In text mode, the text controlled by a given size attribute will be displayed in a different color or brightness to distinguish it from normal text (see COLORS ON SCREEN). In graphics and page modes, WordPerfect will attempt to display the font as it will be printed.

SPECIAL CHARACTERS

Choose Font, Characters (or CTRL+W or SHIFT+F11)
Set, select character set
Characters, highlight a character
Insert

Lets you insert special characters not found on the keyboard from 15 different character sets. Each character is assigned a number: character set, character number, such as 4,5. Be aware that certain monitors cannot display specific special characters, and certain non-graphics printers cannot print specific special characters.

You can also use the Compose feature to insert a special character once you know its WordPerfect Character number. See COMPOSE.

SORT AND SELECT

Choose Tools, Sort (or CTRL+F9)
From (Source): Document on Screen or File
To (Destination): Document on Screen or File
Choose OK
Record Type
Line, Paragraph or Merge Data File
Sort Keys (Sort Priority), establish Criteria, choose OK
Perform Action

Lets you sort lines, paragraphs, merge data files, tables, or parallel columns, as well as select specific records during the sort.

You can block text before beginning the command sequence to sort only a section of a document. Or, position the cursor in a table or parallel columns to sort that element; WordPerfect specifies the record type automatically.

You can sort in alphabetical or numerical order based on a specific word or field in a record. Depending on the type of sort procedure chosen, a record is defined as either a line (line sort), a paragraph (paragraph sort), each group of data ending with an ENDRECORD code (merge sort), or row (table or parallel column sort).

You can also select records that meet particular criteria established for the sort keys.

The default is to sort line-by-line in ascending order (A to Z or smallest number to largest number), based on the first word in each line, and not to select at all. Choose Perform Action to begin the sort assuming the default settings. Change the sort defaults before performing the action by choosing the following items from the Sort dialog box.

- Sort Keys: Defines the characteristics of the word(s) to be used in the sort or in a selection statement, including 1) key (when more than one key is used, the number of the key determines its priority); 2) alphanumeric (sorted by letters and digits) or numeric (sorted by digits only); 3) order (ascending or descending); 4) the line number where the word is found (not for a line sort); 5) the field where the word is found, where a field is identified by the tab stop it is located on (line sort or paragraph sort), or as ending with an ENDFIELD code (merge sort); 6) which word within the field.

  Define more than one key if you wish to sort on more than one word or if you wish to sort on certain words and select on other words. Specify the sort keys first and the select keys last.

- Select Records: Defines a selection statement, the criteria on which text will be extracted, based on the defined keys. For example, if key 1 represented sorting on the zip code in a group of address records, and you wanted to select only the records for the zip code 94901, you would establish the select criteria as Key1=94901. In the selection statement, refer to a key (such as key1 or key2) and use any of the following comparison and logical operators:

=	Equal to	< >	Not equal to
>	Greater than	>=	Greater than or equal to
<	Less than	<=	Less than or equal to
¦	Or		(Either part of the selection statement can be true for a record to be selected)
&	And		(Both parts of the selection statement must be true for the record to be selected)

- Record Type: Specifies whether WordPerfect should sort lines, paragraphs, or records in a secondary merge file.

- View: Allows you to move the cursor up into the text about to be sorted.

When you change any of the sort or select defaults, they remain in effect for subsequent sort procedures unless you change them again or until you exit WordPerfect.

SOUND CLIPS

Plays and records sound clips and adds them to your documents. MIDI or Digital Audio sound files can be used in WordPerfect if your hardware supports them. You can create multimedia presentations or leave a voice message (perhaps some special instructions to an assistant) within a document. It requires a sound card and supporting software driver. If you do not have a sound card in your computer, you will not be able to use this feature.

Creating Sound Clips

Choose Tools, Sound Clip, Record (or CTRL+D)
Select the desired Recording Quality
Rec, begin recording
Stop, Insert

Records a sound clip and inserts it into the document.

Playing Sound Clips

Choose Tools, Sound Clip, Play
Highlight the desired sound clip
Use Play/Pause, Rwnd, Stop, and Ffwd

You can adjust the volume by choosing Volume and typing in a new percentage number, or by using the change buttons located to the right of that option. To play dictation, place the cursor before the sound clip and press CTRL+S. You can begin typing.

Setting Up Sound

Choose Tools (or CTRL+F7)
Sound Clip
Sound Setup
Type
Select correct device name
Hardware Setup

Check the documentation for your sound card to perform the hardware setup. Increasing the sample rate, size, and mode will result in improved sound quality, but will require more memory and disk space. Recording in stereo will double the size of a sound file.

SPELL

Checking a Block

Block the Text
Choose Tools, Writing Tools, Speller (or CTRL+F2)

Spell checks a specific portion of a document on the screen against the main and supplemental dictionaries on disk (see the next section for options when a word is not found in the dictionaries).

Checking a Word, Page, or Entire Document

Choose Tools, Writing Tools, Speller (or CTRL+F2)
Word, Page, Document, From Cursor

Spell checks the document onscreen against the main and supplemental dictionaries on disk. After a page or document spell check, WordPerfect performs a word count. When WordPerfect highlights a word not found in the dictionary, you can select one of the suggested words as a replacement. Or, choose from these other options:

- Skip Once: Ignores this one occurrence of the highlighted word.

- Skip in this Document: Ignores the highlighted word from now on for a spell check in this document only.

- Add to Dictionary: Adds the highlighted word to the supplemental dictionary, so that it will be treated as correctly spelled in any document.

- Edit Word: Allows you to correct the highlighted word with the standard editing keys.

- Lookup: Offers a list of additional words based on a word pattern that you type.

- Ignore Numbers: Tells WordPerfect to ignore all words containing numbers for the rest of this spell check.

- Select Dictionary: Allows you to select a different supplemental dictionary. (One dictionary, WP{WP}US.SUP, is created as your default supplemental dictionary. You can create other dictionaries for special purposes, such as legal or medical supplemental dictionaries. (Select Edit Supplemental Dictionary from the Speller dialog box to create or edit one.)

The speller also pauses at words that appear in an irregular case (such as woRd), and you can choose to skip over the word, edit it, replace it, or disable irregular case checking for the rest of the spell check. It also pauses at words containing numbers.

Looking Up a Word

Choose Tools, Writing Tools, Speller (or CTRL+F2)
Look Up Word
Enter word or word pattern

Looks up words in the dictionary that match a word or word pattern. Enter a word, and WordPerfect displays

options that are phonetically similar. Enter a word
pattern by using ? to represent a single letter and * to
represent any number of letters in succession, and
WordPerfect displays options that fit the pattern.

Using Additional Dictionaries

Choose Tools, Writing Tools, Speller (or CTRL+F2)
Setup (or SHIFT+F1)
Chain Main Dictionaries or Chain Supplemental Dictionaries
Highlight dictionary you want to chain to
Edit
Add to chain

Allows you to base the spell check on more than one
dictionary by adding dictionaries in a chain.

SPREADSHEET

Importing a File

Choose Tools (or ALT+F7)
Spreadsheet
Import
Enter the name of the file to be imported
Range
Spreadsheet or Range (type range address)
Choose Type
Import as Table or Import as Text
Choose Import

Retrieves a spreadsheet file that has been created in
programs such as PlanPerfect, Excel, Lotus, Quattro Pro,
or Quattro Pro for Windows. This is a one-time retrieval,
as opposed to the spreadsheet linking feature (see
"Linking a File").

The options in Import Spreadsheet dialog box are as
follows:

- Filename: The name of the spreadsheet file you wish to retrieve.

- Range: The range you wish to import, which is necessary if you wish to import only a section of the entire spreadsheet.

- Type: Whether to retrieve the spreadsheet as a table or as text formatted into tabular columns.

- Import: Initiates the importing of the spreadsheet file according to the other specifications.

Linking a File

Choose Tools (or ALT+F7)
Spreadsheet
Create Link
Enter the name of the file to be linked
Range
Spreadsheet or Range (type range address)
Choose Type
Import as Table, Import as Text
Choose Link & Import

Creates a link between a spreadsheet file that has been created in programs such as PlanPerfect, Excel, Lotus, Quattro Pro, or Quattro Pro for Windows and a WordPerfect document. The spreadsheet file is retrieved into the WordPerfect document onscreen. (If you prefer, you can establish the link without importing the document by choosing Link instead of Link & Import.)

WordPerfect places link codes and comments in the file. The comments are never printed. The WordPerfect document can thereafter be updated whenever the spreadsheet file is altered. (See "Setting Link Options.")

Setting Link Options

Choose Tools (or ALT+F7)
Spreadsheet, Link Options

Allows you to specify whether links should be
automatically updated when the WordPerfect document
that contains links is retrieved; to initiate links manually
if the updates are not automatic; and to specify whether
the display of link comments that surround the linked
spreadsheets in the WordPerfect document should be
hidden.

STARTUP (SLASH) OPTIONS

Loads WordPerfect and activates one or more special
options at the same time, which can make your work
with WordPerfect more efficient. Sometimes WordPerfect
will not load properly without a startup option. A startup
option takes effect until the next time you load
WordPerfect. Rather than typing wp to load WordPerfect,
type wp/? for a list of available startup options.
Commonly used options are these:

- wp/d=*d*:   Redirects WordPerfect's overflow and temporary files to another drive where *d*: is the drive (such as
  a:, **b:**, and so on). You can specify a RAM drive to speed
  operations, if you wish.

- wp *filename*   Retrieves the file specified as soon as
  WordPerfect is loaded.

- wp/m=*macroname*   Executes the macro specified as
  soon as WordPerfect is loaded.

- wp/nb   Specifies that no .BK! backup file is created,
  even temporarily, when you choose to replace a file on
  disk with the document onscreen.

- **wp/nc**   Disables the Cursor Speed feature, which may conflict with certain equipment or with other software loaded before WordPerfect (see also CURSOR SPEED).

- **wp/nf**   Activates a nonflash option in the event that your screen periodically goes blank or you use a windowing program.

- **wp/nk**   Disables enhanced keyboard commands that may conflict with certain equipment or other software loaded before WordPerfect.

- **wp/ps=***path*   Tells WordPerfect the location of, and your desire to use, a .SET (setup) file that is in a directory other than where the WordPerfect WP.EXE program file is stored.

- **wp/sa**   Allows a network installation to run in stand-alone mode.

- **wp/ss=***rows,columns*   Sets the screen size if WordPerfect is not automatically detecting the correct screen size. Do not exceed the screen size that the video controller is set to display.

- **wp/tx**   Loads WordPerfect in text mode.

- **wp/u=***user initials*   On a network, automatically provides unique WordPerfect ID for individual user's temporary files.

- **wp/x**   Loads WordPerfect and restores the original default settings as defined by WordPerfect Corporation, despite any changes to defaults made with the Setup menu (as described in SETUP).

You can use the DOS SET command in the AUTOEXEC.BAT file to establish any of the startup options as environmental variables. For instance, include SET WP=WP/TX in the AUTOEXEC.BAT file. This will enable you to simply type **wp** to load the program with the desired startup options.

STRIKEOUT

Prints the text with strikeout markings, usually a line
through the text marked for strikeout. Use this text
attribute when you wish to mark characters of text that
could possibly be deleted, without actually deleting the
text.

See APPEARANCE for the command sequence to insert
strikeout manually. See DOCUMENT COMPARE for the
command sequence to have WordPerfect compare two
documents and insert strikeout marks automatically
wherever text in the document on disk does not appear
in the document onscreen.

STYLES

Creating/Editing Styles

Choose Layout, Styles (or ALT+F8)
Position cursor on style name (if editing)
Create or Edit

Defines the combination of formatting codes and/or text
that make up a style, which can then be used to format
elements in a document. Or, edits a previously created
style definition. You can also copy a previously created
style and edit the copy, thus preserving the original. The
following are options when you create or edit a style:

- Style Name: The style name, which will be used when
  you wish to turn a style on or off in the text.

- Description: Describes the formatting task accomplished by the style.

- Type: Specifies whether the style will be character, paragraph, or an open type. Character and paragraph types
  have a beginning and end, while the open type has only
  a beginning and is not turned off.

- Contents: Allows you to insert the codes and text that comprise the style. WordPerfect displays a dialog box. Above the entry field are the code selections that are available for the type of style you are creating/editing.

- Enter: Determines whether, after turning on a style, pressing the ENTER key will insert a hard return, turn off the style, or turn it off and then on again. Pertinent only if you are defining a character or paragraph type of style.

If you select a style in the text (see "Selecting Styles") and then edit the style definition, the text affected by that style will automatically update to reflect the new style definition.

You can also create or edit system styles, which are styles attached to particular features, such as graphics boxes and lines, borders, fill, and outlining. Remember that an edited style will affect all elements on which the style is based.

Deleting Styles

Choose Layout, Styles (or ALT+F8)
Position cursor on style name
Delete

Deletes a previously created style. You must indicate whether you wish to leave the codes, which means the style and the style codes are erased but the text/codes that comprise that style remain in the text; or include the codes, which means the style, style codes, and text/codes that comprise the style are erased.

Selecting Styles

Choose Layout, Styles (or ALT+F8)
Highlight the desired style
Select to turn on the style

A paragraph style is turned off by pressing ENTER (if you defined the ENTER key to turn off the style). Otherwise, repeat the command sequence above to turn off the style.

A character style is turned off by pressing ENTER (if you defined the ENTER key to turn off the style). Otherwise, choose Layout, Styles, Off.

You can also block text before selecting, to turn on a paragraph or character style. The style is applied only to the blocked text.

An open style is turned on but not off; the style affects the text from the current cursor position to the end of the document (or until other codes of the same type are inserted farther forward in the text).

When the cursor is positioned on a style code, the code expands on the Reveal Codes screen to display the text/codes that define the style.

Saving/Retrieving Style Libraries

Choose Layout, Styles (or ALT+F8)
Save or Retrieve
Type filename

Typically, styles are saved along with the document in which they were created. You can, however, save a list of styles into a separate file and then retrieve that list into any other document as a library. (Instead of retrieving a library, you can assign that library to a document and then switch to it; see the next section.)

Working with Style Libraries

Choose Layout, Styles (or ALT+F8)
Personal Library or Shared Library

Switches from a display of styles for the current document to styles in a library. A style library is a group of styles that can be used in any document. Personal libraries are those you put together yourself, while shared libraries are shared by people on a network.

You must specify a location for your default library before you can switch to style libraries. See LOCATION OF FILES for the command sequence. WordPerfect comes packaged with a library named LIBRARY.STY (stored in

C:\WP60 if you installed WordPerfect to that directory), which you can use as the default library.

Once you establish a style library, that list of styles is automatically attached to every new document that you subsequently create. You can also assign a different style library to a document, using Options from the Styles List dialog box.

SUBDIVIDE PAGE

Choose Layout (or SHIFT+F8)
Page, Subdivide Page
Enter number of columns
Enter number of rows

Use to create booklets, programs, cards, or any other type of document that requires logical pages (subdivisions) on a page. Each logical page is separated from the other logical pages with a hard page break (CTRL+ENTER). This feature works very much like the labels feature.

SUMMARY, DOCUMENT

Creating/Editing a Document Summary

Choose File, Summary
Modify options as desired
Press F7

Offers an efficient method for keeping track of the contents and history of a document. The summary is a fill-in-the-blanks form, where information is either inserted by you or by WordPerfect (if you choose Extract or press SHIFT+F10).

Document summary information includes revision date and creation date; descriptive name/type; author/typist; subject, which WordPerfect can insert; account; keywords; and abstract, which WordPerfect can insert as the first 400 characters from the document.

An existing document summary can be viewed or edited by repeating the command sequence. A document summary is displayed when you use the Look feature to view the contents of a file on disk (see LOOK). A document summary can also be used with the Find feature when looking for a document. (See FIND FILES.)

You can view descriptive names and types from the File Manager. When you customize the File Manager setup, choose the Descriptive Names and Types option. (See DESCRIPTIVE NAME.)

When viewing a document summary, choose Delete (or F9) to erase the summary, choose Select Fields (or F4) to change the fields listed in the summary, choose Print (or SHIFT+F7) to print the summary, or choose Save (or F10) to save it into a file.

Setting Up a Document Summary

Choose File, Summary
Setup (or SHIFT+F1)
Subject Search Text, Default Descriptive Type
   or Create Summary of Exit/Save

Sets defaults for the operation of the Summary feature: 1) identifies for WordPerfect the subject search string, which is inserted as the subject of a new document summary when you choose Extract to capture that information; 2) tells WordPerfect whether or not to prompt you for a document summary when you save a document for the first time; and 3) specifies a default descriptive type.

SUPPRESS FOR CURRENT PAGE

Choose Layout (or SHIFT+F8)
Page, Suppress

Suppresses page numbering, headers, footers, and
watermarks for the current page. Useful for suppressing
these features on the first page of a letter or report, or on
a single page containing a table or chart.

TAB ALIGN

Choose Layout, Alignment, Decimal Tab (or CTRL+F6)

Vertically aligns text or numbers on a decimal/align
character at the next tab stop. For example, if the
decimal/align character is the decimal point (period), you
can align a column of numbers on the decimal point. (See
also DECIMAL/ALIGN CHARACTER to learn how to
change this character.)

When WordPerfect prompts "Align char =", type the tab
entry. When the decimal/align character is typed, the
prompt disappears. (If this character is not typed, then
the entry is aligned flush right on the tab stop.)

Choose decimal alignment twice in a row to precede text
with dot leaders (....).

TABLES

Creating Tables

Choose Layout (or ALT+F7)
Tables, Create
Enter number of columns
Enter number of rows

Defines the basic table structure. WordPerfect automatically creates evenly spaced columns in a grid pattern based on the current margin settings. Each intersection of a column and row in the grid is referred to as a *cell*. Cells are labeled alphabetically from left to right in each row (A, B, C, and so on) and numerically from top to bottom (1, 2, 3, and so on) in each column, so that the first cell in the upper-left corner is labeled A1.

Default settings are for double lines to border the outside of the table, single lines to border the inside, and for text within each cell to be left justified. Press F7 when you are done editing the table structure and are ready to type text into the table

Deleting/Inserting Rows or Columns

Position cursor within table
Choose Layout, Tables, Edit (or ALT+F11)
Position cursor on cell in row or column
DEL or INS

Deletes or inserts the number of rows or columns that you specify. If you delete, both the contents of the cells as well as the cells themselves are deleted, unless you choose to delete only the contents. (You can also delete the contents of a block of cells without deleting the actual cells by performing the deletion in the document window instead of the Table Edit dialog box.)

Editing Tables/Performing Math

Position cursor within table
Choose Layout, Tables, Edit (or ALT+F11)

Displays the Table Edit dialog box, allowing you to change default settings for the table structure and to perform mathematical calculations in the table. Before selecting from the Table Edit dialog box, position the cursor appropriately. To alter settings for a single cell, position the cursor on that cell; for a column or row, position the cursor on any cell in that column or row; for a group of cells, use the Block feature to highlight that group. Options on the Table Edit menu include

- Cell: Sets the design characteristics for cells, including the vertical alignment, justification, font attributes, and number format. If no settings are altered, the cell uses the same format characteristics as the column by default.

- Column: Sets the design characteristics for columns, including column width, vertical alignment, justification, font attributes, and number format.

- Row: Sets the design characteristics for the rows including Row Margins, Row Height, the number of lines that can be contained in a row, and whether the table will contain header rows that print on successive pages if the table spans a page break.

- Table: Sets the design characteristics for the entire table, including table position, column margins, vertical alignment, justification, font attributes, and number format.

- Lines: Determines the style of lines around a cell, block of cells, or the table.

- Join: Combines multiple cells from adjoining rows or columns into one cell.

- Split: Splits a cell into multiple cells.

- Formula: Allows you to create spreadsheet-like formulas in a table. Before creating a formula, place the cursor in the cell that should display the result of the formula.

  You can use addition (+), subtraction (−), multiplication (*) or division (/) in a formula. You can use cell references in your formula, just as you can in a spreadsheet program. For instance, if you want to multiply the contents of cell A1 by the contents of cell A2, the formula would be A1*A2.

  Ninety-eight predefined functions, including very sophisticated functions used for financial analysis, logical operations, and comparison operations are available. To create a formula using a function and a range of cells (for instance, if you are trying to arrive at a sum for cells A1 through A15), choose Functions (F5), highlight the desired function ("Sum" in the case of the example), and choose Insert (the function is then placed in the formula field). If the function requires arguments (in this case, the names of the cells containing the values you wish to sum), type the arguments between the parentheses that follow the function's name. To complete the example formula, the arguments would consist of the beginning cell address (A1) followed either by a colon (:) or two periods (..), then the ending cell address. The resulting formula would be "Sum(A1:A15)."

You can copy a formula from one cell to others, where all cell references in that formula are copied relatively. Or select from three math operators for calculating down a column:

+	Subtotal
=	Total
*	Grand Total

Once you insert formulas in a table, choose Calc from the Tables Edit dialog box to recalculate formulas if you edit values in the table.

Moving/Copying Cells

Choose Layout (or ALT+F7)
Tables, Edit
Block the cells or position cursor
  in the row or column
Move/Copy
Block, Row, Column, or Cell
Move or Copy
Reposition cursor
ENTER

Moves or copies one cell, a block of cells, a row, or a column. For a block, text is moved or copied into preexisting cells and overwrites the contents of those cells. For a row or column, a new row or column is created when it is moved or copied.

Typing Text in Cells

You can type text into cells in any order. When the cursor is located in a table, the status line contains a cell indicator, for example:

Cell A1   Doc 1   Pg 1   Ln 1.14"   Pos 1.12"

After typing text into a cell, use the arrow keys to move the cursor to the next cell in the arrow's direction, or press TAB to move to the next cell and SHIFT+TAB to move to the previous cell. Also, see the "General Reminders" section for methods to move the cursor in a table.

Working with Floating Cells

Choose Layout (or ALT+F7)
Tables
Create Floating Cell or Edit Floating Cell
Name, Type name or accept the suggested name
Number Type, Select the desired number type
Formula
Create formula

A floating cell is used to reference cells in a table or other floating cells in a document. The floating cell is made up of paired codes. Place a formula between the paired codes to return a value from a table or another floating cell.

TABLES OF AUTHORITIES

Defining Tables of Authorities

Choose Tools, Table of Authorities
Define, Create
Type a name for the Table of Authorities

Make other desired modifications:
Style, Numbering Mode (3-7), Page Number Format
Combine Sequential Page Numbers and Underlining
Allowed

Defines the location and style options for one section of a table of authorities (citations) when it is generated. You can define up to 16 sections for a table of authorities. Once you specify a section number, a Table of Authorities Definition screen appears for that section, offering the following style options: whether page numbers, which will appear flush right, should be preceded by dot leaders; whether to allow underlining; and whether blank lines should be inserted between authorities.

You can also edit or delete a definition, or retrieve a file of definitions. Moreover, choose Setup (or SHIFT+F1) to set default options.

Generating Tables of Authorities

Generates a table of authorities after you have marked the text for the table and defined the table. Up to 16 sections of the table of authorities can be generated, one for each table of authorities definition mark inserted in the document. (See GENERATE CROSS-REFERENCES, INDEXES, LISTS, AND TABLES for the command sequence.)

Marking Text for Tables of Authorities

For full form:

Block the text
Choose Tools (or ALT+F5)
Table of Authorities,
Mark Full
Enter section name
Enter short form
Edit Full Form

For short form:

Choose <u>T</u>ools (or ALT+F5)
Table of <u>A</u>uthorities,
Mark <u>S</u>hort
Enter short form

Marks the citation you wish to be included in a table of authorities when generated. The full form method is used the first time you mark a citation in a document; how you type and edit the full form is how that citation will appear in the table of authorities. The short form method is used for the second and all future occurrences of that citation. The full form and short form for the same citation are linked together with the same short form text.

You can also edit the full form, short form, or section number after marking an authority by choosing <u>T</u>ools, Table of <u>A</u>uthorities, <u>E</u>dit Full.

TABLES OF CONTENTS

Defining Tables of Contents

Choose <u>T</u>ools, Ta<u>b</u>le of Contents
<u>D</u>efine
<u>N</u>umber of Levels, Table of Contents <u>S</u>tyle,
   Level Style, Numbering <u>M</u>ode, <u>W</u>rap
   Last Level, and <u>P</u>age Numbering Format

Defines the location and style options of the table of contents when it is generated. When you follow the command sequence, a Table of Contents Definition screen appears, offering style options for how many levels the table will contain, whether or not the last level will be wrapped, and which numbering style will be used when the table is generated. Wherever the cursor is located when you follow the command sequence is where the table of contents will appear when generated.

Generating Tables of Contents

Generates a table of contents after you have marked the text for the table and defined the table (see GENERATE CROSS-REFERENCES, INDEXES, LISTS, AND TABLES for the command sequence).

Marking Text for Tables of Contents

Block the text
Choose Tools, Table of Contents
Mark
Enter table of contents level number

Marks the word or phrase you wish to be included in a table of contents when generated.

TABS

Setting Tabs

Choose Layout, Tab Set (or CTRL+F11)
Choose Absolute or Relative
Set tabs on tab ruler

Changes the location of tab stops and is used to change where the first line of a paragraph is indented, or to design a chart of aligned text/numbers. A ruler line shows the current tab stop locations. Procedures are as follows:

- To erase the current tab stops from the cursor to the end of the tab ruler line, choose Clear All (CTRL+END). To delete one tab stop, position the cursor and choose Clear One (DEL).

- To set evenly spaced tab stops, choose Set Tab, type the starting position, choose Repeat Every, and type the increment measurement. For evenly spaced tab stops, WordPerfect assumes the left-justified style unless the starting position contains a tab of another style.

- To set an individual tab, move the cursor to the desired location on the tab ruler or enter the number representing the location. Then choose Left, Right, Center, or Decimal. Choose Dot Leader only if you want a line of dots to precede the tab location.

Tabs can be set in either of two ways: relative type or absolute type. *Relative* means that the tabs are set relative to the left *margin,* so that tab locations adjust to remain the same distance from the left margin if the left margin setting is changed. *Absolute* means that tabs are set absolute with respect to the left *edge* of the paper form, and not the left margin, so that the tab locations stay fixed if the left margin setting is changed.

Using Tabs

TAB key

Positions the cursor at the next tab stop. If the next tab stop is

- Left: All text typed on that tab stop to the end of that line is aligned against the tab stop.
- Right: All text is aligned flush right against the tab stop.
- Center: The text is centered over the tab stop.
- Decimal: The decimal (or other decimal/align character) typed as part of the entry is aligned on the tab stop.

If the tab style has a dot leader, a row of dots will display from the point where you pressed the TAB key up to the tab stop.

If you press HOME before pressing TAB, you can left align text at the next tab stop regardless of the style of tab setting. Moreover, other keys in addition to TAB operate on tab stops to align text in different ways. (See BACK TAB, DECIMAL/ALIGN CHARACTER, and INDENT.) If you press HOME before pressing either SHIFT+F6, ALT+F6, or CTRL+F6, you can insert a center, right, or decimal-aligned tab at the current tab setting regardless of the style of that tab setting.

TABULAR COLUMNS

See TABS to set or use tab stops for creating tabular columns. *See* SELECT for procedures to delete, cut, and copy tabular columns.

TEXT COLUMNS

Defining/Turning on Text Columns

Choose Layout, Columns
Column Type
Newspaper, Balanced Newspaper, Parallel,
    or Parallel with Block Protect
Modify the other options as desired:
    Number of Columns, Distance Between
    Columns, Line Spacing Between Rows,
    and Column Borders

Defines and turns on the column layout. You define from 2 to 24 columns, choosing one of four types: newspaper, where text flows down a column all the way to the bottom of the page and then starts at the top of the next; balanced newspaper, where column length is adjusted so that all columns are of equal length; parallel, where related text remains together in short, adjacent columns across the page; and parallel with block protect, which are similar to parallel columns except that no column entry will be split by a page break.

When the cursor is located in a portion of the document where column mode is on, the status line contains a column indicator, for example:

Col 1   Doc 1   Pg 1   Ln 1"   Pos 1"

Moving the Cursor Between Text Columns

See the "General Reminders" section.

Typing Text in Newspaper Columns

Type complete text

Formats text into the newspaper-style column layout that you defined. You can define your columns and turn columns on before typing the text, or afterwards.

When a page's bottom margin is reached, the cursor moves to the top of the next column so you can continue typing. When a page's bottom margin is reached in the last column, the cursor moves to the top of the first column on the next page.

To end a column before the bottom margin is reached, insert a HARD PAGE by pressing CTRL+END; the cursor moves to the top of the next column or to the top of the first column on a new page.

Typing Text in Parallel Columns

Type text of one short, adjacent column
HARD PAGE (CTRL+ENTER)

Formats text into the parallel-style column layout that you defined. Be sure to define your columns and turn columns on before typing the text.

Each group of adjacent columns across the page is typed before continuing with the next group of adjacent columns. WordPerfect automatically inserts a blank line between each group of parallel (adjacent) columns.

See also TABLES as an alternative to parallel columns.

Turning Off Text Columns

Choose Layout, Columns
Off

Turns Column mode off if it was on.

TEXT/GRAPHICS QUALITY

Choose File, Print/Fax
Text Quality or Graphics Quality
Do Not Print, Draft, Medium, or High

Determines the quality level with which text and/or graphics will be printed. This is useful to print out draft copies quickly or to print out text and graphics in separate printings (for printers that cannot print text and graphics in the same print job or that don't have sufficient memory to print both at once). The higher the quality, the better the resolution on the printed page and thus the longer it takes for the printer to complete the print job. Be aware that for some printers, the menu items Draft, Medium, and High have no effect on the output.

THESAURUS

Position cursor on word
Choose Tools, Writing Tools (or ALT+F1)
Thesaurus

Provides synonyms and antonyms for the highlighted word. Use the arrow keys to move the cursor within the list of synonyms and antonyms and between the three columns of words displayed. The following options are available on the Thesaurus menu:

- Look Up: Allows you to look up synonyms and antonyms for another word.

- View: Allows you to move the cursor up into the text to peruse the document before making a word selection.

- <u>C</u>lear Column: Clears the list of synonyms and antonyms for the last word selected.

- <u>H</u>istory: Provides a list of the headwords you have looked up.

- <u>R</u>eplace: Substitutes the word corresponding to the letter you select for the highlighted word.

- Cancel: Exits from the Thesaurus.

THOUSANDS SEPARATOR

Choose <u>L</u>ayout (SHIFT+F8)
Cha<u>r</u>acter, <u>T</u>housands Separator

Alters the character used to separate the thousands digits when using the Math or Tables feature (see also MATH COLUMNS and TABLES). The default is the comma.

TYPEOVER MODE

INS key

In Typeover mode, characters you type will replace (type over) existing characters. INS is a toggle switch, which shifts the way WordPerfect edits text between Insert and Typeover modes. The initial setting is Insert mode (see also INSERT MODE). In Typeover mode, the message "Typeover" appears on the status line.

UNDELETE

<u>E</u>dit, <u>U</u>ndelete (or ESC)
<u>R</u>estore or <u>P</u>revious Deletion

If no menu or prompt is on the screen, recovers any of the last three deletion levels, where a deletion level is a group of consecutive deletions. A deletion level is shown highlighted at the current cursor position.

The Restore menu item reinserts the highlighted text at the current cursor position, while the Previous Deletion menu item shows another of the last three deletion levels as highlighted text.

UNDERLINE

Produces characters that are underlined when printed. In text mode, the underlined text can be displayed on the screen in a different color or brightness, to distinguish it from normal text, or with an actual underline. (See also COLORS ON SCREEN to set the way that the underline attribute is displayed onscreen.) In graphics or page layout modes, the text will be underlined.

To alter the way in which the Underline feature operates, see UNDERLINE SPACES AND TABS.

For Existing Text

Block the text
Font, Underline (or F8 or CTRL+U)

The Underline attribute will be applied only to the text in the block.

For Text About to Be Typed

Font, Underline (or F8 or CTRL+U) to turn on underline
Type the text
Font, Underline (or F8 or CTRL+U) to turn off underline

When you turn off the Underline feature, the cursor is moved to the right of the "Underline Off" code. In addition to using the menu commands or pressing F8 or CTRL+U, as described above, you can also tap the RIGHT ARROW key.

UNDERLINE SPACES AND TABS

Choose Font, Font (or CTRL+F8)
Underline
Spaces and/or Tabs

Determines how underlining will appear on the printed page. You can request that WordPerfect underline spaces, tabs, both spaces and tabs, or neither spaces nor tabs that are between a beginning and ending underline code.

UNDO

Choose Edit, Undo (or CTRL+Z)

Reverses the effect of the last editing maneuver. You can only undo the last editing action. Repeat the command sequence twice to cancel the "undo".

UNITS OF MEASURE

Choose File, Setup (or SHIFT+F1)
Environment, Units of Measure
Display Entry of Numbers and Status Line Display

Alters the way measurements are displayed in two circumstances: on the status line, and for features that require a measurement entry (such as margins, tabs, line height, and so on). Your options include inches (either " or i), centimeters (c), millimeters (m), points (p), 1200ths of an inch (w), or WordPerfect 4.2 vertical and horizontal units (u).

Regardless of the measurement you select as the default, you can enter measurements in a different unit. After typing the number measurement, type in a letter that indicates the unit you are using. For example, you can indicate a specific margin as 1.5" (inches), 2.5c (centimeters), or 90p (points). WordPerfect will convert your entry into the default unit of measurement.

VIEW MODES

See the "General Reminders" section

WATERMARK

Choose Layout, Header/Footer/Watermarks
Watermarks
Choose Watermark A or Watermark B
All Pages, Even Pages or Odd Pages
Create (places you in the Watermark editor)
Either type headline text or create a graphics
   image to print behind the document text
Press F7 to return to the document window

Places headline text or a graphics image behind the document text. It can be used to create a design element in your document or to place messages like "Draft," "Important," and "Confidential" on the page. The feature works much the same way as headers and footers. You can have two watermarks, which can alternate between odd and even pages, if you wish. (See GRAPHICS BOXES for instructions on inserting a graphics image as a watermark.)

WIDOW/ORPHAN PROTECTION

Choose Layout, Other
Widow/Orphan Protection

Ensures that one line of a paragraph is not stranded on a
separate page due to a soft page break. With
Widow/Orphan Protection turned on, a page break may
occur one line earlier or one line later to keep the first or
last line together with the rest of the paragraph.

WINDOWS

Lets you work with up to nine documents at one time, as
long as your computer has sufficient memory. Use the
Open feature or the New Document feature to open
additional document windows. (See OPEN DOCUMENT
and NEW DOCUMENT.) Use the Close feature or the Exit
feature to close document windows. (See CLOSE
DOCUMENT and EXIT DOCUMENT.)

Cascading and Tiling Windows

Choose Window
Cascade or Tile

Allows you to manage the display of the open document
windows. Cascade arranges the documents in a
cascading fashion so that the title bar of each open
window is displayed. Tile splits the screen so that each
open window can be seen.

Framing a Window

Choose Window
Frame

Places the document window in a frame and displays the
onscreen controls for the window.

- Title bar: Displays the name of the document.

- Sizing border: The border surrounding the window can be used to move or resize it with a mouse. Drag the top border (title bar) to move it. Drag any of the other borders to resize.

- Exit button: Dot in the upper-left corner. Allows you to exit from the active document using a mouse.

- Minimize button: Down arrow in the upper-right corner of the screen, which can be used with a mouse.

- Maximize button: Up arrow in the upper-right corner of the screen, which can be used with a mouse.

Once a frame surrounds a window, the window can also be sized or moved with the keyboard. Press CTRL+F3 and choose Window, Move or Window, Size. Then use the cursor movement keys. Press ENTER when you're done moving or resizing.

Minimizing/Maximizing Windows

Choose Window
Minimize or Maximize

Minimize reduces the window to a medium-sized rectangle. Maximize expands the window so that it covers the entire screen, eliminating any frame. With a mouse, you can also minimize and maximize a window with the buttons in the upper-right corner of the frame.

Switching Between Multiple Document Windows

Choose Window, Switch To (or F3)
Select the desired document window

Lists all the open windows, letting you move the cursor between the open document windows. The selected window becomes the active one. The status line indicates which document is on the screen.

To switch between the currently active window and the last active window, you can choose Window, Switch (or SHIFT+F3).

You can also cycle through all the open windows. Continue to press CTRL+Y. Or, choose Window, Next or Window, Previous.

Using a mouse, you can also switch to any window that is in view by clicking on that window.

WORD AND LETTER SPACING

Choose Layout (or SHIFT+F8)
Other, Printer Functions
Word/Letter Spacing
Word Spacing or Letter Spacing
Normal, Optimal, % of Optimal, Set Pitch

Adjusts the spacing between adjacent words and letters. Options include Normal (spacing that looks best according to the printer manufacturer), Optimal (spacing that looks best according to WordPerfect Corporation), Percent of Optimal (enter a percentage—numbers less than 100 percent reduce the spacing), and Set Pitch (enter a pitch in characters per inch).

WORD SPACING JUSTIFICATION LIMITS

Choose Layout (or SHIFT+F8)
Other, Printer Functions
Word Spacing Justification Limits

When justification is full, determines how much WordPerfect expands or compresses spacing between words to justify a line. Once a spacing is reached

between words, WordPerfect adjusts the spacing
between characters.

WORDPERFECT CHARACTERS

See SPECIAL CHARACTERS

ZOOM

Choose <u>V</u>iew (or CTRL+F3)
<u>Z</u>oom
<u>5</u>0%, <u>7</u>5%, 100<u>%</u>, 125%, 15<u>0</u>%, <u>2</u>00%, <u>3</u>00%, <u>M</u>argin
   Width, Page <u>W</u>idth, or <u>F</u>ull Page

Allows you to specify the magnitude of your view of a
document onscreen. Zoom is only active for graphics and
page mode. Using CTRL+F3 allows you to zoom to 800
percent. Margin Width displays the complete document
from left to right margin. Page Width displays the
complete width of the document; the font onscreen will
be resized to reflect the correct ratio to the page width
(this does not affect printing). Full Page allows you to see
how the text will be laid out on the entire page.

INDEX

D

H

I

J

K